AI ART
MACHINE VISIONS AND WARPED DREAMS

Joanna Zylinska

The **MEDIA : ART : WRITE : NOW** series mobilises the medium of writing as a mode of critical enquiry and aesthetic expression. Its books capture the most original developments in technology-based arts and other forms of creative media: AI and computational arts, gaming, digital and post-digital productions, soft and wet media, interactive and participative arts, open platforms, photography, photomedia and, last but not least, amateur media practice. They convey the urgency of the project via their style, length and mode of engagement. In both length and tone, they sit somewhere between an extended essay and a monograph.

Series Editor: Joanna Zylinska

AI ART
MACHINE VISIONS AND WARPED DREAMS

Joanna Zylinska

OPEN HUMANITIES PRESS

London 2020

First edition published by Open Humanities Press 2020
Copyright © 2020 Joanna Zylinska

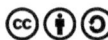

Freely available at:
http://openhumanitiespress.org/books/titles/ai-art/

This is an open access book, licensed under Creative Commons By Attribution Share Alike license. Under this license, authors allow anyone to download, reuse, reprint, modify, distribute, and/or copy their work so long as the authors and source are cited and resulting derivative works are licensed under the same or similar license. No permission is required from the authors or the publisher. Statutory fair use and other rights are in no way affected by the above. Read more about the license at creativecommons.org/licenses/by-sa/4.0/

Cover Art, figures, and other media included with this book may be under different copyright restrictions.

Print ISBN 978-1-78542-086-3
PDF ISBN 978-1-78542-085-6

OPEN HUMANITIES PRESS

Open Humanities Press is an international, scholar-led open access publishing collective whose mission is to make leading works of contemporary critical thought freely available worldwide.
More at http://openhumanitiespress.org/

Contents

Acknowledgements 7

AI (and) Art: An Introduction 11

1. A So-Called Intelligence 23
2. The Ethics of AI, or How to
   Tell Better Stories about Technology 29
3. Why Now? AI as the
   Anthropocene Imperative 39
4. 'Can Computers Be Creative?':
   A Misguided Question 49
5. Artists, Robots and 'Fun' 57
6. The Work of Art in the
   Age of Machinic Creation 65
7. Generative AI Art as Candy Crush 75
8. Seeing like a Machine,
   Telling like a Human 87
9. Undigital Photography 105
10. An Uber for Art? 117
11. From Net Art and Post-Internet Art to Artificially
    Intelligent Art – and Beyond 129
12. AI as Another Intelligence 137

Future Art, Art's Future: A Conclusion 145

(Art) Gallery of Links 155

Notes 161

Works Cited 165

Acknowledgements

Several events gave impetus to the emergence of this book. The 2017 edition of the Ars Electronica festival in Linz, Austria, held under the banner of 'AI: Artificial Intelligence / Das Andere Ich', served as its original inspiration – and provocation. I am extremely grateful to the organisers for the invitation to present at the festival symposium and to see the artworks, many of which featured, or engaged with, AI. I am also much indebted to Daria Parkhomenko from the LABORATORIA Art & Science Space in Moscow, for asking me to speak about the renewed interest in AI in art as part of the conference 'Daemons in the Machine: Methods for Creating Technological Art', held at the British Higher School of Art and Design in March 2018. Last but not least, the opportunity to serve as a jury member and keynote speaker at the awards ceremony for P3 prize, focusing on collaborative and interdisciplinary developments in the field of post-photography and organised by Fotomuseum Winterthur at The Photographers' Gallery in London in May 2018, allowed me to crystallise the skeleton of my argument that went to on become this book, while also planting the seeds of the visual project which accompanies it.

Sections of the book have subsequently been trialled at the Royal College of Art, Prague's FAMU, the University of Applied Arts in Vienna (Die Angewandte), Ben Gurion University of the Negev, Vassar College, international photography festival Photoszene Cologne, Berlin's Internet and digital society conference re:publica, University of Manchester's Whitworth Gallery, Pratt Institute, Trinity College Dublin and Tekniska museet in Stockholm. I am grateful for all the invitations, the generous engagement with my work in all of those places – and the new ideas and directions all those visits sparked off.

I am very grateful to the artists who have generously shared their work with me, in particular Katja Notivskova, Leonel Moura, Guido Segni and Mike Tyka. I owe a special debt to Mario Klingemann for his eloquence, patience and generosity of spirit in engaging and humouring me at the various platforms we have shared over the recent years, especially when I raised issues with AI-driven art. My biggest debt of gratitude is to the legion of Amazon's MTurk workers, whose 'artificial artificial intelligence' – as Amazon unironically puts it – is responsible for the more critical direction this book has ended up taking.

Many individuals have helped me develop and fine-tune the ideas contained here. I would especially like to thank Giovanna Borradori, Tomas Dvorak, Nea Ehrlich, Beate Gütschow, Alex Grein, Greg Hainge, Anne Kaun,

Acknowledgements 9

Marco de Mutiis, Maja Ozvaldic, Jussi Parikka, Luke Skrebowski, Katrina Sluis, Nick Thurston and my PhotoLab colleagues at Goldsmiths (Clare Bottomley, Alice Dunseath, Jacob Love, Damian Owen-Board, Daniel Rourke). A final huge thank-you, for all sorts of things, is owed to Gary Hall, Sigi Jöttkandt, David Ottina and Lisa Blackman.

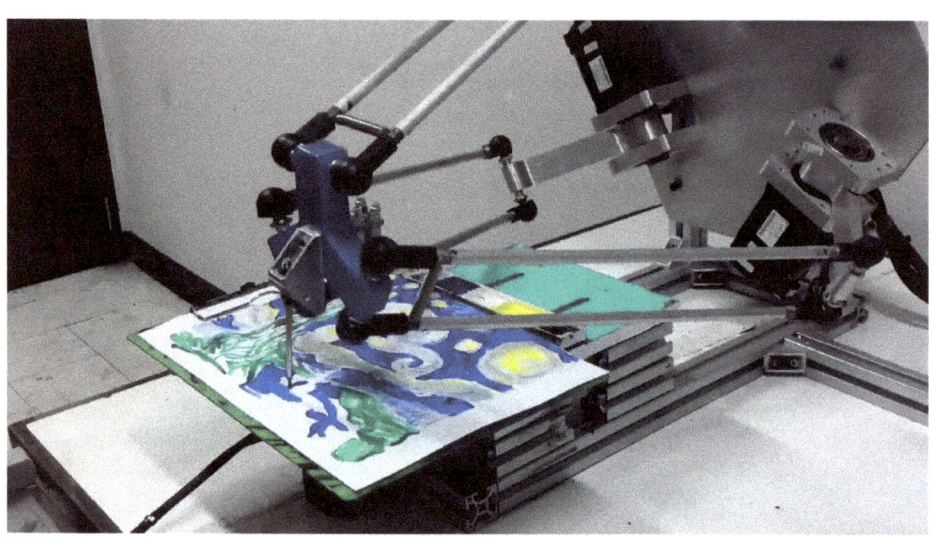

Fig. 1. Screenshot from *ReART: The Starry Night (Part 2)*, Robot Art 2017, CMIT Robotics, Kasetsart University.

AI (and) Art: An Introduction

The annual Robot Art competition launched by Internet entrepreneur and dating-websites founder Andrew Conru invites 'visually beautiful' paintings made by robots. The winners so far include a dot-painted portrait of Albert Einstein, a copy of *The Starry Night* by Vincent van Gogh that took a robot four hours and fifty minutes to produce (fig. 1) and a series of pictures executed by a programme called CloudPainter. Written by Pindar Van Arman, CloudPainter enables a 'style transfer' from the work of an established artist, as a result of which we get pictures which look like they could have been painted by Cézanne or Francis Bacon, but it can also make its own stylistic interventions. In August 2017 Taryn Southern, a self-defined 'artist/futurist with more than 700 million online views', launched a song from what she claimed would be the world's first AI-composed music album.[1] Having fed parameters such as mood, tempo and genre into the open source software called Amper, Southern then overlaid the AI-created instrumentation and chord structure with the lyrics and vocal melodies of her own. In July 2018 the electronics manufacturer Huawei held a photographic competition that was judged by photographer Alex Lambrechts – and a Huawei P20 Pro AI smartphone. Building on its previous claims that the Huawei P20 was equipped with 'Master AI' which automatically set the most optimum camera mode for every situation as well as learning to adapt to user behaviour (Huawei 2018), the Chinese 'AI-powered' flagship was not just making photos but also evaluating them, 'using its artificial intelligence to rate thousands of images alongside a professional Leica photographer'.[2] This recent outpouring of computer-made creative artefacts has been taking place against the unfolding of public interest in artificial intelligence, from fascination with its creative capabilities to anxiety related to the impending automation of the labour force or even the possible annihilation of the human species. The stories and claims regarding (supposed) machinic creativity that accompany the emergence of those artefacts are at least as interesting as the artefacts themselves.

This short book discusses the relationship between artificial intelligence and art in a way that goes beyond the oft-posed question: 'Can computers be creative?'. An attempt to answer this question will nonetheless be made, together with demonstrating why this may not be *the best question* to ask about AI-driven art. Along the way, I will formulate many alternative and largely open-ended questions, in an attempt to challenge the binary strictures of much of the current thinking on AI. Yet questioning will not be the only thing I'll do. The book's argument will take the form of a critique, but this should not be treated as a technophobic rejection of AI art, or AI itself. On the contrary, I am deeply intrigued by the technical and cultural possibilities of AI, and by the claims and promises made in its name by developers, investors and commentators. But I want to offer a more nuanced position on understanding our relationship with technology. Instead of pitching the human against the machine, I propose to see different forms of human activity, including art, as having *always* been technical, and thus also, to some extent, artificially intelligent. My critique will primarily focus on the political underpinnings of the current AI debate and the way it feeds into art, although I will have some acerbic things to say about certain forms of AI-driven aesthetics. The exploration of the issue of machine vision in current AI research will lead me to raise broader questions about different ways of seeing, (in)visibility and perception, across various platforms and scales. Last but not least, I will seek to recognise the potential of AI art for breaking the circuit of what philosopher Franco 'Bifo' Berardi has called neurotalitarianism (2017) and for enabling a different form of psychopolitics.

AI Art has been shaped by a number of broader questions with regard to art, media and technology: Is there an ontological difference between early computer-generated art, net art and the more recent forms of AI-driven art? Or is it just a difference of degree, i.e. of the mode and intensity of technological entanglement? Should the recent applications of AI to image making and image curating encourage us to (re)turn to bigger questions concerning the very purpose of artistic production? What are art, photography and other forms of image making *for*? *Who* are they for? Does art exist outside the clearly designated realm of human cultural practice? Will AI create new conditions *and* new audiences for art? What will art 'after' AI look like? Who will be its recipient?

While the book's argument may seem to be more explicitly focused on the question of production – the production of AI-driven art itself and the production of technological and conceptual frameworks *for* such art – the problem of art's reception inevitably reoccurs throughout. Indeed, *AI Art* ultimately considers the socio-political and psycho-political stakes of redesigning the artistic apparatus, with all its production and display institutions – from art schools and artists' studios through to galleries and festivals – for the public at large. In recognising that the reception of technological art, especially of the kind that uses or at least engages with AI, requires some degree of technical competency, it asks what is being unveiled and obscured by the current artistic discourse around AI. Going beyond aesthetic experience and the sense of 'fun' that is often associated with technology-driven art, it considers art's role in demystifying new technologies while highlighting some socio-political issues – but it also explores the limitations of art as a debunker of techno-hype.

The very notion of 'AI art' posited in the book's title is a proposition, not a typological designation. This is why I veer between the visually more straightforward 'AI art' and the more descriptive and instrumental-sounding 'AI-driven art'. But my principal ambition is not to lock us to a definition but rather to stage a conceptual and disciplinary encounter between two concepts – 'art' and 'artificial intelligence' – which themselves have rather fraught legacies and valences, and which both face uncertain yet intriguing futures. And thus I approach 'art' from a post-art-historical position of media theory, building on discussions around conceptualism, technological practice, and social and institutional critique. The analysis of the technological aspect of art is an important factor in this framework, as is the recognition of the social and material conditions in which art is produced and recognised *as art*. This approach supersedes the analysis of the art object as a singular entity with a supposedly timeless value, with a more relational understanding of art's production, reception and recognition in specific socio-historical contexts. Questions of originality and of the genius of an individual producer are hence framed by a study of the wider context that produces conditions for the emergence of a particular art form – and that produces particular audiences which can identify, interpret and engage with that art form. These questions are therefore framed through what Michel Foucault has called an 'author function' (1992, 306): a wider discursive arrangement that stabilises into what a given cultural moment perceives as an 'author' or 'artist'.[3] Aesthetic issues are still under consideration here, but they are seen as being always intertwined with broader questions about cultural and monetary value – and with the way such value is shaped and then frequently passed off as natural. In light of all this, I acknowledge the foundational role of art history and art theory for the emergence of this multidisciplinary cluster of practices and pedagogies that has recently been recognised under the (already wobbly and dual) umbrella term of media art/s (Grau 2007, Paul 2008). Yet, as Oliver Grau argues in the Introduction to his field-defining tome *MediaArtHistories*, 'For the interests of media art it is important that we continue to take media art history into the mainstream of art history and that we cultivate a proximity to film, cultural and media studies, and computer science, but also to philosophy and other sciences dealing with images' (2007, 5). *AI Art* is situated at this cross-disciplinary conjuncture mapped out by Grau.

Eschewing the more rigid organisation typical of a scholarly monograph, the book navigates between the need to introduce material, especially as far as the philosophical and technical aspects of AI are concerned, and the ambition to say something new about the nexus of AI and art. To do this, it adopts a funnel-like structure that takes readers from wider contextualisation to specific issues concerning AI and art, to then open up again, from the other end, to some larger and future-facing questions. It starts from the position that, to understand the promise of AI for the creative fields, we must not remain *just* in the realm of aesthetics. Indeed, I will argue that AI art can realise this promise, or fail to do so, precisely when it engages with broader issues around creativity, intelligence, perception and the role and position of the human in the world – including questions of labour, robotisation and the long-term survival of the human species.

Following on from this introduction, the book engages with wider debates about AI – from offering a critical overview of the very concept of intelligence (chapter 1), through to raising ethical questions about AI (chapter 2). It also attempts to locate the current turn to, or even hype about, AI understood as Artificial Intelligence in relation to *another AI*, which I call the 'Anthropocene Imperative', and which stands for the need to respond to the planetary climate crisis (chapter 3). Starting to narrow down, the argument then moves on to consider the idea of creativity as applied to machines (chapter 4), while also tracing some historical predecessors of robot and machine art (chapter 5). Chapters 6-8 engage more explicitly with artistic productions that draw on AI: from generative art that uses neural networks through to AI's more conceptual applications in the work of artists such as Trevor Paglen and Lauren McCarthy. It is here that the question of machine vision as not just a technical but also a political problem is addressed most directly. The book then offers a case study from the area of computational photography. Looking at issues around automated creativity and labour, it presents a project from my own art practice titled *View from the Window*, a project which offers a perspective on the interlocking of machine intelligence and human labour (chapters 9-10). From chapter 11 onwards

AI Art opens up again to wider artistic and conceptual issues, while also speculating about yet another form of AI art, called here *art for Another Intelligence* (chapter 12). The book's conclusion returns to the questions raised in this introduction to offer speculation on future art, and on art's future, including the exploration of what a truly post-human art would look like – and to whom it would look this way.

The above summary provides a more conceptual account of the book's ins and outs. But there is also an affective dimension to the book. *AI Art* is driven by my passion for the constantly evolving field of art, with all its disciplinary pluralities, kinships and transgressions – and for a domain of technology through which we become in and with the world. Coming as I do from the mixed background of continental philosophy, cultural and media studies, and art practice, I understand *tekhnē* as a constitutive fabric of human and nonhuman life, which manifests itself in human activities such as writing and art, but also in all sorts of technological inventions and interventions – some of which are enacted by the human in ensemble with machines, or are even led by nonhuman forms of intelligence. This is why I am keen to reiterate that my starting position in this book is by no means technophobic. Indeed, I am deeply interested in all sorts of 'cool things we do with computers' (New Scientist 2017) – incidentally, a phrase proposed by Roger Schank, Emeritus Professor of Computer Science at Northwestern University to describe more accurately what goes under the name of AI today. At the same time, I want to interrogate the philosophical assumptions and cultural blind spots behind the current AI discourse and the promises it entails, especially as this discourse relates to image making, art and so-called creativity more broadly.

Indeed, 'so-called' is one of these qualifiers that should be inserted into most pronouncements about AI, starting from the very notion of intelligence (fig. 2). It is because intelligence is actually something of a blind spot of the AI field, with its foundational concept either taken for granted without too much interrogation or moulded at will and then readjusted depending on the direction the research has taken. While some scholars define intelligence as the ability to think in abstract terms, to learn from experience, to adapt to a complex environment or to 'make the right decision in uncertain circumstances' (New Scientist 2017), others are wary of providing a strict definition of this term and rely instead on descriptors such as that 'intelligence is computable' (Barrat 2013, 163).[4] New ground for thinking about intelligence in relation to computation was paved in the 1950s by Alan Turing, for whom the determination of whether a given system was intelligent was to be made purely on the basis of its behavioural capacity, i.e. its being able to do something (or not) (Turing 1950). Multiple definitions notwithstanding, the majority of scholars working in AI today agree on the materialist foundations of intelligence, 'in at least the minimal sense of supposing that matter, suitably selected and arranged, suffices for intelligence' (Haugeland 1997, 2).

This understanding drives many of the present-day efforts to recreate its operations in a different medium than that of a carbon-based body. The next chapter will look at how we have arrived at this present moment – and at what we have allowed ourselves to overlook on the way.

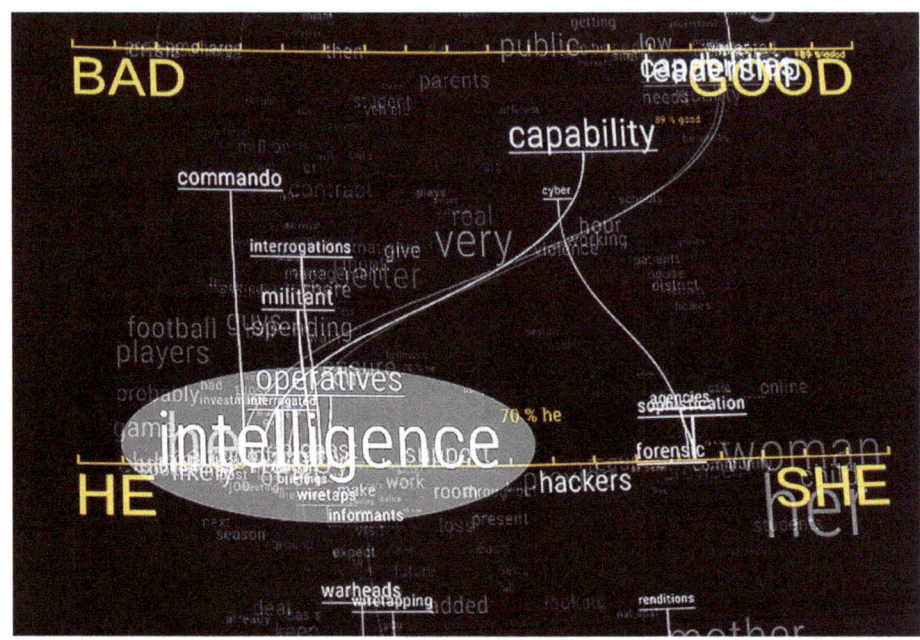

Fig. 2. Joanna Zylinska, photo of my interaction with Google PAIR's project *Waterfall of Meaning* at the Barbican Centre exhibition AI: More than Human (June 2019). The project offers 'a poetic glimpse into the interior of an AI, showing how a machine absorbs human associations between words' (Google Arts & Culture 2019). On entering the word 'intelligence' into the system, I saw it float between the mobile word clouds (in white) and the fixed word pairs (expensive – cheap, bad – good; in yellow), only to swerve decisively towards the large yellow HE when approaching the binary pronoun pairing. The movement of the words in this installation is the outcome of 'word embeddings', i.e. linguistic and cultural associations humans have developed over time with regard to particular words and their contexts – and which the PAIR algorithm has learnt to follow and map out.

CHAPTER I

A So-Called Intelligence

This chapter starts by looking at the historical antecedents of the notion of artificial intelligence and at the research it has spawned. The roots of AI can be traced back to Aristotle's work on formal logic: more specifically, the syllogism, i.e. a form of deductive reasoning that allows one to reach a conclusion derived from a number of statements with an assumed truth-value. Yet the actual research into AI only took off in the 1950s, when scientists and engineers suggested that formal logic could be applied not just by humans but also by machines – and when machines were powerful enough to undertake these kinds of operations of symbolic reasoning. Much work at the time was driven by the desire to enable machines to think *like* humans, a criterion that later became known as the Turing Test. However, 'by the 1980s AI researchers realized that they had neither sufficient hardware nor the knowledge to simulate everything a human can do – and the field fragmented. Instead of working towards one single human-equivalent computer intelligence, research groups splintered off to investigate specific aspects of the larger problem: speech recognition, computer vision and probabilistic inference – even chess' (New Scientist 2017). Enthusiasm and funding slowly petered out and so by the early 1990s research in the field came to a halt in most places, marred by many disappointments and unrealised promises.

Yet over the last decade we have entered what some are calling AI 2.0. The renewed interest in AI research has been accompanied by a change of tack: from what became known as Artificial General Intelligence, whose goal was to replicate the human's mental functioning as such, to specialised, or 'narrow' AI, focused on performing particular tasks and solving singular problems. The new approach involves developing artificial neural networks, 'which at a rudimentary level imitate the way neurons in the brain work', as well as genetic algorithms, 'which imitate genetic inheritance and fitness to evolve better solutions to a problem with every generation' (New Scientist 2017). It also entails perfecting what has become known as 'deep', or 'machine' learning, which is not the kind of learning premised on understanding, but which rather involves being trained in making quicker and more accurate decisions on the basis of analysing extremely large data sets. AI engines learn in the sense that they get better with experience at performing the task they have been trained to perform. The relative success of this new wave of AI – as evidenced in Amazon's recommendation algorithms, the autocomplete function on mobile phones, face recognition, the ability of Google's neural network launched in 2012 to identify cats' faces in videos, or the victory of Google's AlphaGo software over the South Korean master of the complex board game Go, Lee Se-dol, in 2016 – can be explained by adjusted expectations, coupled with a massive increase in computational power. Much of what passes off for AI today is really a product of coupling big data with statistical analysis. Impressive or even mysterious as some of the outcomes may look, they are the result of advanced calculations performed on large quantities of data.

New AI is therefore first and foremost a sophisticated agent of pattern recognition: a post-cyberpunk incarnation of William Gibson's character from his eponymous 2003 novel in which advertising consultant Cayce Pollard had an almost superhuman ability to make connections and find meanings within the flow of marketing data. Interestingly, current popular entertainment has seen an increased presence of human characters who excel at pattern recognition and who, in a reverse scenario that reveals how popular culture deals with current fascinations, desires and anxieties with regard to technology, end up being able to emulate AI 2.0: we can think here of pretend Harvard Law School graduate Matt Ross from USA Network's legal drama TV series *Suits*, nerdy hacker Mr Robot from USA Network's series of the same name or time travelling ex-soldier Takeshi Kovacs equipped with the capacity for total recall from Netflix's *Altered Carbon*. In its ability to use 'brute force computation', (what-looks-like) AI is indeed capable of achieving goals that can delight, surprise or even shock us humans. Fast computational power coupled with the availability of large data sets has led to significant advances in machine learning, a development which has led scientists such as Ray Kurzweil (2005) to predict the imminent era of singularity in which humans will merge with machines to achieve one unified, and by then disembodied, intelligence – coupled with immortality. Nick Bostrom has upped the ante with his book *Superintelligence* (2014), in which he criticises Kurzweil's concept of singularity for not only being imprecise but also for sounding techno-utopian. Bostrom argues that the construction of machines whose power considerably and radically supersedes that of human brains will have dramatic consequences. Rather than focus just on the arrival of an AI that matches human intelligence, he explores what he calls an intelligence explosion, a more radical and intense development that will 'swoosh right by' humanity. For Bostrom, 'This is quite possibly the most important and most daunting challenge humanity has ever faced. And – whether we succeed or fail – it is probably the last challenge we will ever face' (2014).

The resurfacing of the hubristic narratives about human futures spurred on by the latest AI research has been accompanied by the excavation of the myth of the robot (and its cousins, the android and the cyborg) as the human's other, an intelligent companion who can always turn into an enemy – such as HAL 9000 from *Space Odyssey* or the killer robotic dog from season 4 of *Black Mirror*. Popular imagination has thus once again been captured by both salvation narratives and horror stories about 'them' taking over 'us': eliminating our jobs, conquering our habitat and killing us all in the end. Such stories, be it in their salutary or horror-driven guises, are premised on a rather unsophisticated model of the human as a self-enclosed non-technological entity, involved in eternal battle with *tekhnē*. However, humans are quintessentially technical beings, in the sense that we have emerged with technology and through our relationship to it, from flint stones used as tools and weapons to genetic and cultural algorithms. Instead of pitching the human against the machine, shouldn't we rather see different forms of human activity as having always relied on technical prostheses and forming part of technical assemblages? Does this perspective change the story in any way? Does it call for some better stories – and better questions?

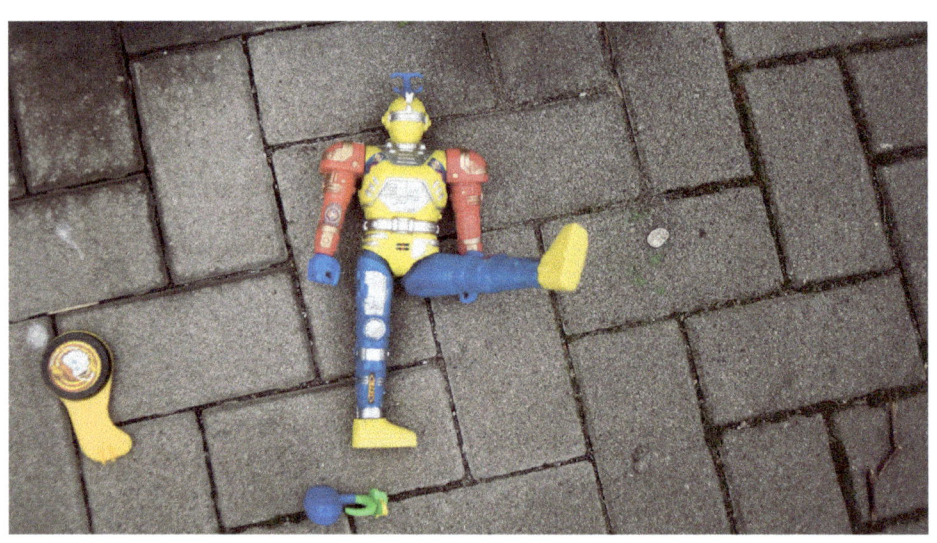

Fig. 3. Joanna Zylinska, raw footage from *Exit Man*, 2017.

CHAPTER 2

The Ethics of AI, or How to Tell Better Stories about Technology[5]

To recognise humans' kinship with technology, and thus potentially with AI, is not to say that all forms of AI are created equal (or equally benign), or that they may not have unforeseen consequences. It is rather to make a plea for probing some of the claims spawned by the dominant AI narrative – and by their intellectual and financial backers. This acknowledgement repositions the seemingly eternal narrative of the human's battle against technology as an ethico-political problem, one that needs to be investigated under given social conditions. The specific questions that need to be asked concern the modes of life that the currently available AI algorithms enable and disable: Whose brainchild (and bodychild) is the AI of today? Who and what does AI make life better *for*? Who and what *can't* it see? What are its own blind spots? Artists, mediamakers and writers can help us search for answers to these questions by looking askew at the current claims and promises about AI, with their apocalyptic as well as redemptive undertones – and by retelling the dominant narratives in different genres and media (fig. 3). Storytelling and other forms of art making may even be the first step on the way to ethical, or responsible, AI.

One key reference point in contemporary discussions of AI ethics are Isaac Asimov's Three Laws of Robotics:

1. A robot may not injure a human being or, through inaction, allow a human being to come to harm.
2. A robot must obey orders given it by human beings except where such orders would conflict with the First Law.
3. A robot must protect its own existence as long as such protection does not conflict with the First or Second Law. (1950, 40)

What is most interesting about Asimov's laws is not so much the codification of behaviour they prescribe to his narrative creations but rather the fact that his 'robot ethics' is part of fiction. Developed in several short stories and published in the 1950 collection, *I Robot*, Asimov's ethical precepts are mechanical, reductive and naively humanist. First of all, they are premised on a rather restricted idea of the robot as the human's truncated, and inherently obedient, other. Like many other forms of deontological (i.e. normative) moral theories, they constitute an elegantly designed ethical system which works as a moral parable but fails in real-life scenarios when those precepts are put to the test.

It is because humans often act in an impulse-driven, robotic manner, when making, in a split second, what are meant to be ethical decisions: e.g. when rescuing a drowning child, intervening in a fight or deciding whether to shoot while flying over supposed enemy targets. Also, humans are not only partly robotic but quite glitchy too. At some point they are thus bound – through stupidity, malice or sheer curiosity – to introduce noise and error into Asimov's perfectly envisaged rational scenarios and creations.

Yet Asimov was no moral philosopher and so to turn his laws into a standalone moral proposal is to do a disservice to the imagination and creative potential of his stories. What needs commending instead is Asimov's very gesture of *doing ethics as/in fiction*, or even his implicit proposition that ethical deliberation is best served by stories, rather than precepts or commandments. This is why I want to suggest that one of the most creative – and most needed – ways in which artists can use AI is by *telling better stories about AI*, while also *imagining better ways of living with AI*. Reflecting on the nature of this double 'better' would be the crux of such artistic endeavours. Mobilising the tools of imagination, visualisation, narrative, metaphor, parable and irony, artists can perhaps begin by blowing some much-needed cool air on the heat and hype around AI currently emitting from tech companies. To propose this is not to embrace a technophobic position or promote a return to narrative forms of yesteryear: detached, enclosed, single-medium based. It is rather to encourage artists to use their technical apparatus with a view to exposing the blind spots behind the current AI discourse. Art as a technical activity can thus channel the Greek origins of the term *tekhnē*, referring as it does both to technical assemblages such as computers, databases and neural nets and, more crucially perhaps, to the very process of bringing-forth, or creation. It can also usefully highlight the fact that, for ancient Greeks, there was no distinction between art and technology. Laurence Bertrand Dorléac goes back even deeper in time to highlight this ontological link when she points out that 'Starting from the prehistoric caves, artists have remained connected to their technical environment, whose tools they always appropriate to invent new forms' (2018, 15). Interestingly, the very concept of *art*ificial intelligence is premised on artifice, which in its Latin etymology (*artificium*) goes beyond the current meaning of deception and trickery to signal art, craft and skill.

When thinking about adequate responses to ethical issues raised by AI, we should also listen to some more sceptical voices coming from the AI community. Andrew Ng, a computer scientist at Stanford University and former chief scientist at China's Internet giant Baidu, said in 2015: 'I don't work on preventing AI from turning evil for the same reason that I don't work on combating overpopulation on the planet Mars' (New Scientist 2017). In *Life 3.0: Being Human in the Age of Artificial Intelligence* cosmologist Max Tegmark points out that the reason for this restraint is primarily temporal, as it will be quite a while until we are able to build an

Artificial General Intelligence (AGI) which poses a significant threat to the existence of the human species. (Some AI engineers *do* worry about this threat, as we will see in the next chapter.) Yet to worry about it now, claims Tegmark, would serve as a detraction from the current research into the field. Tegmark also points out that the dismissal of such fears as unwarranted is one of the very few things the majority of AI researchers actually agree on, although they cannot even pinpoint what this 'quite a while' would stand for, with utopians believing AGI will arrive within the next twenty to a hundred years and techno-sceptics pointing to centuries. Tegmark believes that, when AGI does eventually arrive, engineers will already have found a solution: a so-called 'beneficial AI' whose goals will supposedly be aligned with those of humans. The fact that, over centuries, humans have not managed to align their goals with one another when it comes to such fundamental issues as the value of human (and nonhuman) life, and that they have in fact created and embedded political systems that are fundamentally premised on value differentials when it comes to life, seems to escape many of the well-meaning AI thinkers.

By borrowing from Andrew Ng's scepticism with regard to the supposed existential threat posed by AI, I am not by any means advocating that we abandon criticality: only that we assess more realistically the current stage of technological research and the claims made in its name. This will also need to involve accepting that traditional moral paradigms, with their religiously inflected, transcendent notions of good and evil, cannot be unproblematically applied to AI issues. The problem here is with our age-old humanism, which draws on culturally constructed values it then passes off as universal, while also veiling the very act of their construction, with all the power mechanisms involved in the process. When it comes to AI, such an application of traditional moral theory, with its discrete rational subject, is also most likely going to be futile – as well as intellectually inadequate – given that it frames the AI agent as a mere extension of the human, without allowing for the possibility that AI's intelligence may take the form that is not only superior to that of the human, but also unrecognisable by humans *as intelligence.* (We have already failed the intelligence recognition test with regard to octopi, as the illuminating book, *Other Minds: The Octopus and the Evolution of Intelligent Life* by Peter Godfrey-Smith, indicates.) Traditional moral theory with its disembodied rational moral subject is actually inadequate in many, perhaps most, other cases where no AI is involved.[6] This is why I want to suggest that, alongside artistic modes of engagement, many of the problems currently discussed under the umbrella of 'AI ethics' would be much better served by policy discussions, with that old-school mode of intervention, regulation, offering a more pragmatic way of countering some of the failures of the ethics discourse. This is especially important in light of the fact that ethics is often just mobilised as a rhetorical and legal smokescreen aimed at getting the industry 'off the hook', with companies hiring moral philosophers and virtue-signalling their attachment to 'ethical values' while trying to overcome national-level legislation and societal expectations. Any meaningful discussion of AI ethics therefore needs to take place in a wider socio-political context, rather than a purely procedural one.

Contrary to the majority of AI researchers discussed by Tegmark who claim we should not 'worry' about AI now because, when the time to worry comes, we will have already come up with a technofix, I believe that interesting and imaginative discussions about AI could not be more timely. This is why my argument in this book joins the already unfolding conversation about the aesthetics, ethics and politics of AI to address the relationship between AI and art, or more broadly, AI and creative activity in different media, *right here right now*. Even if the current technology only allows us to call present-day creations 'prefigurative AI art' – because, according to Tegmark, no one seriously believes that 'proper AI' is going to happen any time soon (which is why many scientists and engineers tend to avoid the all-catch term 'AI' and prefer to use more precise terms such as 'machine learning', 'natural language processing' or 'computer vision') – *something is already happening*. This 'something', which is a confluence of technical and cultural changes, industry claims, popular anxieties, moral panics and creative interventions across different media and platforms, demands our attention, I suggest. I thus take Ng's declaration that he doesn't work on preventing AI from turning evil for the same reason that he doesn't work on combating overpopulation on Mars as a call for rhetorical and conceptual restraint, but also for imagining better narratives about AI, beyond horror stories and fairy tales.

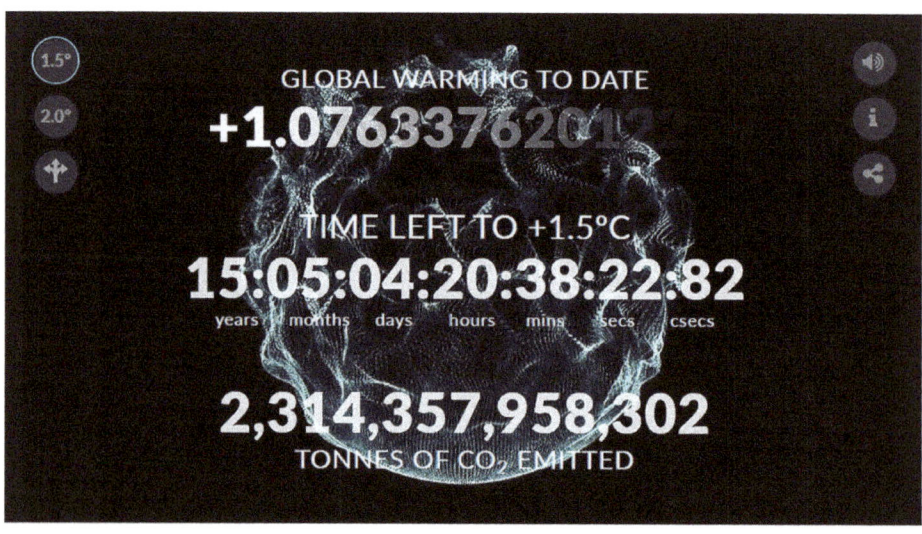

Fig. 4. Screenshot of the Reimagine AI's / Human Impact Lab's *The Climate Clock*, showing the status quo on June 27, 2019, at 11:28 GMT, https://climateclock.net/.

CHAPTER 3

Why Now? AI as the Anthropocene Imperative

Intriguingly, Mars is precisely where many Silicon Valley entrepreneurs plan to relocate in order to avoid the imminent threat of overpopulation, the shortage of resources and the ecological disasters brought on by climate change. I would go so far as to suggest that the renewed interest in AI on the part of Silicon Valley researchers and investors is a response, although not necessarily a direct or even acknowledged one, to a number of planetary-scale issues associated with the Anthropocene.[7] The Anthropocene as a new geological epoch during which human impact upon our planet has been described as being both stratigraphically significant and irreversible has become one of the dominant crisis narratives our times. It has led not only to an increased awareness of environmental issues across the globe but also to a concerted effort to develop effective forms of ecological consciousness and ecological praxis which are meant to help repair the planetary damage. The Anthropocene narrative reveals how the belief in seemingly interminable growth has led to depletion, scarcity and the crisis of biological and social life. This revelation prompts a reflection on what we can do about the crisis we have at least partly authored. In this context, I would like to propose we see AI as standing not just for Artificial Intelligence but also for the Anthropocene Imperative: a call to us humans to respond to those multiple crises of life while there is still time.

My view is that Silicon Valley fails spectacularly in responding to this imperative: the discourse of extinction brought on by the awareness of the Anthropocene merely results in a desire on the part of many AI researchers and investors to reverse-engineer extinction via AI, to Make Man Great Again (Zylinska 2018). Extinction is understood by them not to be the result of anthropogenic climate change, or even of an irreversible course of natural history, but rather as a technical problem to be solved. Even if, as argued earlier, we have nothing to 'worry' about right now, this lack of worry does not mean that intelligent machines will not eventually pose a threat to the human species. The robotically-framed discourse of extinction has made its way into current AI thinking, with apocalypticism competing against the rosier visions of human-machine unity, and against ideas about imminent technofixes. In a biographical note on himself penned in the third person in 1998, mathematician I. J. Good, who 'had served as chief statistician in Alan Turing's code-breaking team in World War II' (Bostrom 2014) and whose work had been foundational to much of AI research, abandoned his earlier technooptimism to convey his horror about the AI explosion. The note proclaimed:

> [The paper] 'Speculation Concerning the First Ultraintelligent Machine' (1965) ... began: 'The survival of man depends on the early construction of an ultraintelligent machine'. Those were his [Good's] words during the Cold War, and he now suspects that 'survival' should be replaced by 'extinction'. He thinks that, because of international competition, we cannot prevent the machines from taking over. He thinks we are lemmings. (cited in Barrat 2013, 117)

Significantly, the present-day capital-fuelled human thinking on AI itself manifests a rather narrow set of intelligence markers, which are premised on a truncated, disembodied and yet so-very-gendered model of human subjectivity. There is therefore something rather dry about current AI research and the promises that drive it – not in the sense that it is too dense, complex or even perhaps too intelligent to be written about in an exciting way. That is certainly not the case. AI research is dry, I suggest, because it is premised on hydrophobia, i.e. wariness of the material or, better, *elemental* side of media technology.[8] Even though doomsday scenarios offered by certain AI gurus – like the claim by sci-fi author and mathematics professor Vernor Vinge that 'The threat landscape going forward is very bad. We're not spending enough effort thinking about failure possibilities' (cited in Barrat 2013, 123) – sound like they would be referring precisely to the climate crisis, their focus, as is the case with Vinge, is much narrower: they are merely pointing to designing ourselves into *extinction by AI*. A strangely unified 'we' is evoked in such narratives, positing the whole of humanity as both culprit and victim of AI, with computational research understood as a kind of multiuser arms-race game.

Pulling themselves up by the bootstraps of their own capital, shooting cars into space while planning to relocate to a secure bunker in New Zealand once a disaster strikes (see O'Connell 2018), many Silicon Valley visionaries seemingly remain blind to the encroaching reality of a different form of deluge than the currently experienced data flood: a literal overflow that awaits most coastal regions in the world. As reported by *The Guardian* in 2016,

> Technology giants including Facebook and Google face the prospect of their prestigious Silicon Valley headquarters becoming swamped by water as rising sea levels threaten to submerge much of the property development boom gripping San Francisco and the Bay Area. Sea level forecasts by a coalition of scientists show that the Silicon Valley bases for Facebook, Google and Cisco are at risk of being cut off or even flooded, even under optimistic scenarios where rapid cuts in greenhouse gas emissions avoid the most severe sea level increases. (Milman 2016)

It may seem disingenuous to position the renewed rise of interest in AI, aka Artificial Intelligence, as a replacement problem for the other AI that I have been foregrounding here under the rubric of the Anthropocene narrative. But I am not trying to suggest that the AI research community manifests any *explicit* climate change denial. The claim I am making is that the direction, tenor and focus of the current AI research *make this research look like a displacement activity* with regard to the planetary issues concerning our climate and, ultimately, our survival, with climate change presented as being ultimately fixable by technology. The still very gendered engineering mindset that shapes the AI field is wedded to what I referred to in my earlier work as masculinist solutionism (see Zylinska 2014, 2018). The imagined solutions involve nuclear fission, designed to provide alternative energy sources to fossil fuels, or geoengineering, in the form of injecting carbon into the soil or deflecting solar radiation by installing mirrors in space. Such solutions are currently being discussed in some quarters as viable fixes to the climate problem, while also reassuring investor-speculators about the continued support for growth economy. Combatting climate change as such is therefore seen as less urgent by the majority of investors than combatting robots. At the foundational meeting in 2014 of the Future of Life Institute, which Tegmark co-leads with, among others, Skype founder Jaan Tallinn, and whose Scientific Advisory Board includes Nick Bostrom and Elon Musk, 'There was broad consensus that although we should pay attention to biotech, nuclear weapons and climate change, our first major goal should be to help make AI-safety research mainstream' (Tegmark 2017). Tegmark justifies this conclusion by arguing that 'In comparison with climate change, which might wreak havoc in fifty to two hundred years, many experts expect AI to have greater impact within decades – and to potentially give us technology for mitigating climate change' (2017). Given that there is much actual evidence of climate change affecting life on our planet *here and now* and not in some kind of remote future, and that any exploration of the threats posed to humanity by AI is mainly speculation at this point – partly because we do not yet *have* AGI – it is hard to avoid a conclusion that AI researchers just prefer to turn their eyes away from the Anthropocene Imperative. Put crudely, it looks like it is simply more fun to continue playing their computer game(s).

Token gestures such as lending help to AI-driven artistic projects about climate change do not alter the wider trend and direction of the current AI research. Indeed, works by outfits such as the Montreal-based creative studio Reimagine AI, who list Google, Autodesk and the 'Good Anthropocene' promoters Future Earth as their 'partners and collaborators', actually end up reinforcing the misguided message that *time is on our side*. Reimagine AI's *The Climate Clock* (fig. 4), projected as a sequence of digits enclosed in an orbit, visualises global warming by showing the time left until the world's temperatures rise in a way that will have a significant impact upon life on our planet (14 years for a 1.5°C rise, 27 – for a 2.0°C rise at the time of writing). Their *Rising*

Seas, in turn, is an interactive 3D platform that 'allows users to visualize and understand the real impacts of sea level rise at specific iconic public locations'.[9] Such visualisations can ultimately have a mollifying effect because they replace the *horror vacui*, i.e. the possibility of the disappearance of life as we know it – which the human sensorium is seemingly unable to grasp fully, notwithstanding popular culture's fascination with apocalyptic tropes – with a series of palatable images, digits and graphs.

But things do not have to be this way. Artists could take the Anthropocene Imperative more seriously than the Valley-based investors and researchers do by expanding the range of survival scenarios beyond the technofixes that include the de-extinction of the vanished species, space colonisation and an intelligence race against robots. AI-driven art that responds responsibly to the Anthropocene Imperative could thus help us expand the current imaginary, allowing for the emergence of new visions and vistas for the world to come. *Shapeshifting AI* and *Shadow Glass*, two projects by the intersectional feminist collective voidLab included as part of the 'Feminist Climate Change: Beyond the Binary' exhibition put together by the School of the Arts and the Department of Design Media Arts at UCLA at the 2017 Ars Electronica: Festival for Art, Technology and Society may show us the way, at least conceptually. In their installations which remix human voice, ambient sound and 3D animation, the artists have created an eerie environment for taking on political questions concerning algorithms, with their current forms of oppression and othering. Both Reimagine AI and voidLab engage with AI primarily on a rhetorical level: theirs are not AI art projects as such, but rather computer-based works that mobilise AI as their theme and concept, with a view to contributing to the debate about human and nonhuman futures, on our planet and beyond. While Reimagine AI ultimately domesticate the AI threat, voidLab explore its weird edges in an attempt to politicise it. 'Alienation has been a source of power for those who have already been alienated in society', the machinic voiceover in the *Shapeshifting AI* video, which cuts up an interview with writer Nora Khan, proclaims. By introducing a rift within the seamless concept of 'humanity' that underpins much of current AI thinking, with its sense of a unified species sporting unified goals, it shifts the parameters of the AI debate beyond the naïve 'us' and 'them' dyad. voidLab's projects do not count as AI art but rather as *art about AI*, but they manage to raise poignant questions about the narrow concept of 'us' in AI research. With that, they pave the ground for a more critical engagement with the very terms of the AI debate.

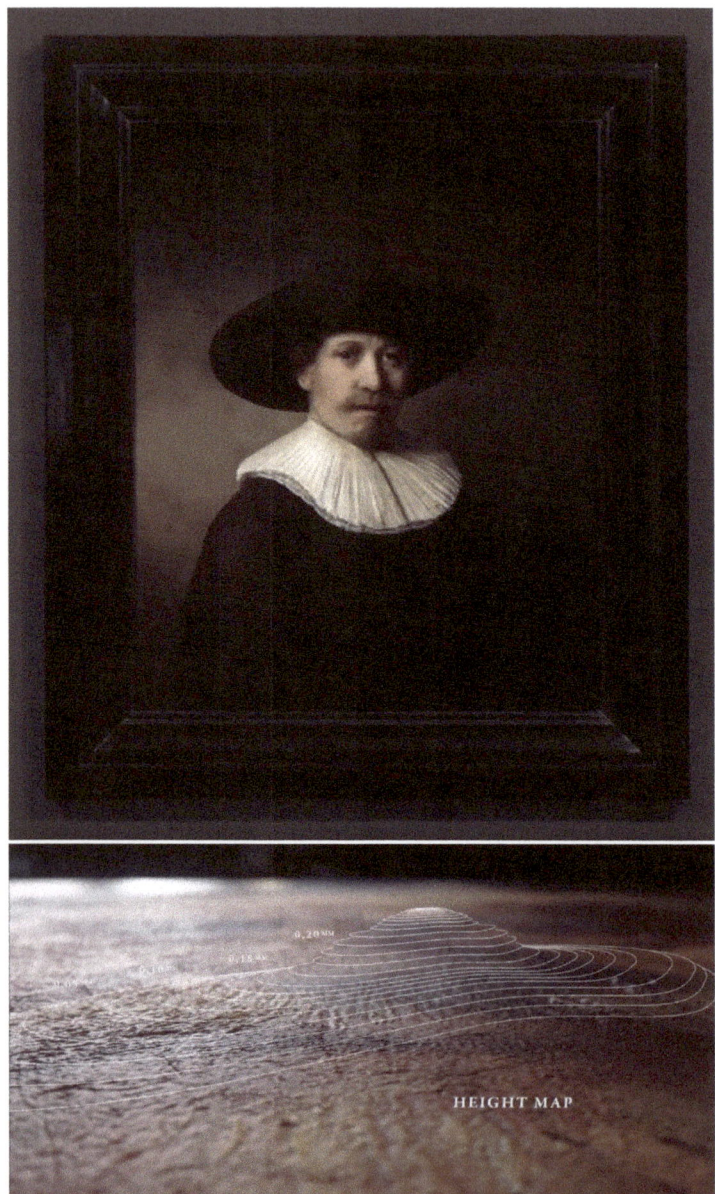

Figs. 5a-5b. Screenshots from *The Next Rembrandt* video, ING / Microsoft 2016.

CHAPTER 4

'Can Computers Be Creative?': A Misguided Question

While mainstream AI researchers bury their heads in virtual sand that will be of no use once the sea levels rise, much of what passes for AI-driven art, especially of the industry-sponsored variety, remains quite superficial, even if visually captivating. The projects that gain most public attention are those that embrace AI rather instrumentally, with aesthetics reduced to things looking 'beautiful', i.e. symmetrical, mesmerising, garish, and, first of all, similar to what already exists. Even some of the more thoughtful engagements with the creative side of AI principally understand art – be it music, painting, or literature – in terms of structure and pattern, with subsequent diversions from the established code and canon being treated as creative interventions. The more critical understanding of art in terms of the creation of new forms of expression with a view to saying something different about the world, or actually intervening in it, is ignored for the sake of what we might term 'crowd-sourced beauty', a rebooted version of 'I know what I like'. Creativity, another term regularly used to brand such works and declare their success, is reduced here to the repetition of the same. This mechanism is revealed most explicitly in the public and, inevitably, curatorial fascination with what we may call 'AI imitation work', also known as 'style transfer'. This mode of artistic production departs from the classical conceptualisation of art in terms of mimesis, i.e. the imitation of nature and its representation. For Aristotle, *all* art was mimetic, but mimesis, proceeding by addition and not just repetition, involved what we would today call a 'remediation' (Bolter and Grusin 2002) of nature. It was thus a form of creative engagement, although one that was not yet linked to the humanist notions of originality and genius. Unlike mimesis, 'style transfer' is pure mimicry: a belaboured resemblance which is also a masquerade. In the context of the AI industry, where much of this kind of mimicry art is being produced, we need to ask: what underpins those efforts and what is it they actually attempt to masquerade as?

In 2016 a projected dubbed *The Next Rembrandt*, led by Microsoft in collaboration with private and public institutions, garnered significant attention worldwide (figs. 5a-5b). A painting seemingly looking like it had come from under the brush of the Dutch master was unveiled in Amsterdam. Featuring a white gentleman with facial hair, wearing dark clothes with a white collar and a hat, and positioned against a dark background, it was based on the results of a deep learning algorithm analysing over 300 scans of the existing works by Rembrandt and coming up with their most characteristic features. The data obtained was then transformed into a new image and 3D-printed with ink that simulated oil paint, to offer realistic-looking texture and depth. Hitting all the keys in the rhetorical register of AI art, Microsoft proudly declared: 'it is a visualization of data in a beautifully creative form. It is a powerful demonstration how data can be, "... used to make life itself more beautiful"'.[10] The 'Can it pass?' question posed in relation to AI-based art which is modelled on the existing historical canons, genres and individual artists' styles receives a lot of public and media attention for a number of reasons. First, it shows up patron- and market-driven conventions based on the supposed aura of the master and (usually) *his* uniqueness as manufactured. Artist Joseph Rabie has suggested in a posting to the nettime mailing list that 'a Rembrandt-painting computer is no more than an algorithm, devised by talented programmers who have enabled it to "teach itself" the rules allowing it to mimic the painter. This is not art, but the empirical science of perception being modelled and applied at a high level'.[11] Yet this supposedly scientific notion of perception, tied as it is to the expert idea of art, is precisely what tends to rile the general public. Imitation art thus encourages populist sneering at experts, who may end up being 'taken in' by an artificially generated van Gogh or Bacon. Last but not least, this kind of guessing game with regard to the provenance of an AI-generated piece is seen by many as good fun, a point to which I will return later on.

These imitation experiments in AI thus open up an interesting debate about our conventionally accepted parameters of authorship, originality, expertise and taste. *New Scientist* has raised an important philosophical point with regard to simulation works such as *The Next Rembrandt* and its kin: 'If it is so easy to break down the style of some of the world's most original composers into computer code, that means some of the best human artists are more machine-like than we would like to think' (2017). A similar line of thinking has been offered by philosopher of technology Vilém Flusser, who argues that humans in the industrial society exist in a close-knit relationship with their apparatuses, which are more than old-style tools such as hammers, scythes or paintbrushes that operate on matter. Instead, contemporary apparatuses consist of machines, the software they run on as well as their wider infrastructures, with their multi-level operations enacting symbolic as much as material transformations.

The human's relationship with technology is not one of enslavement, even if Flusser does raise serious questions for the humanist notion of agency. Yet he also recognises that machinic entanglement facilitates new kinds of action, which he deems collaborations. He goes so far as to suggest that 'This is a new kind of function in which human beings are neither the constant nor the variable but in which human beings and apparatus merge into a unity' (Flusser 2000, 27). Flusser is writing about photographers, evoking the camera as a quintessential modern apparatus that takes human labour beyond the sphere of pure toil and into what we might call playful co-creation, yet his argument arguably extends to other forms of human creativity. Humans' creative activity is understood by Flusser as an execution of the machine's programme and involves making a selection from the range of options determined by the machine's algorithm. We could suggest that this algorithmic relationship which humans depend on is not only actualised in the post-industrial society, even if it does take a particular form and turn at that time, but rather that it has been foundational to the constitution of the human as a technical being – who actuated this humanness in relation with technical objects such as fire, sticks and stones (see Simondon 2016, Stiegler 1998). Humans' everyday functioning also depends on the execution of a programme: a sequence of possibilities enabled by various couplings of adenine, cytosine, guanine, and thymine, i.e. DNA. As I argued elsewhere,[12] this proposition should not be taken as a postulation of a mindless technological or biological determinism that would remove from humans any possibility of action as artists, critics or spectators – and any responsibility for the actions we take. Yet accepting our affinity with other living beings across the evolutionary spectrum and recognising that our human lives are subject to biochemical reactions that we are not fully in control of, *does* undermine the humanist parameters of the debate about creativity, art and AI. Flusser's concept of a 'programmed freedom' is premised on the recognition that, while 'the apparatus functions as a function of the photographer's intention, this intention itself functions as a function of the camera's program' (2002, 35).

Disallowing a strict division between humans and robots, our (supposed) genius and artificial intelligence, such a post-human view of the human recalibrates human creativity as partly computational. Once again, to say this is not to resign ourselves to passivity by concluding that humans are incapable of creating anything, that we are nothing but clockwork devices responding to impulses. It is only to concede, after Flusser, that, just as the imagination of the apparatus is greater than that of all artists across history,[13] the imagination of 'the programme called life' in which we all participate, and which is an outcome of multiple processes running across various scales of the universe, far exceeds our human imagination. To understand how humans can operate within the constraints of the apparatus that is part of us becomes a new urgent task for a (much needed) post-humanist art history and art theory. In this new paradigm for understanding art, the human would be conceived as part of the machine, dispositive or technical system – and not its inventor, owner and ruler. A post-humanist art history would see instead all art works, from cave paintings through to the works of so-called Great Masters and contemporary experiments with all kinds of technologies, as having been produced by human artists *in an assembly with a plethora of nonhuman agents*: drives, impulses, viruses, drugs, various organic and nonorganic substances and devices, as well as all sorts of networks – from mycelium through to the Internet. The frequently posed question, 'Can computers be creative?', which I promised to address in this book, therefore reveals itself to be rather reductive because it is premised on a pre-technological idea of the human as a self-contained subject of decision and action. The 'computer', be it in the shape of a data-processing machine, a robot or an algorithm, is only seen here as an imperfect approximation of such a human. But, in light of the argument laid out here, we should rather be asking, after Flusser, whether *the human* can actually be creative, or, more precisely: *in what way* can the human be creative?

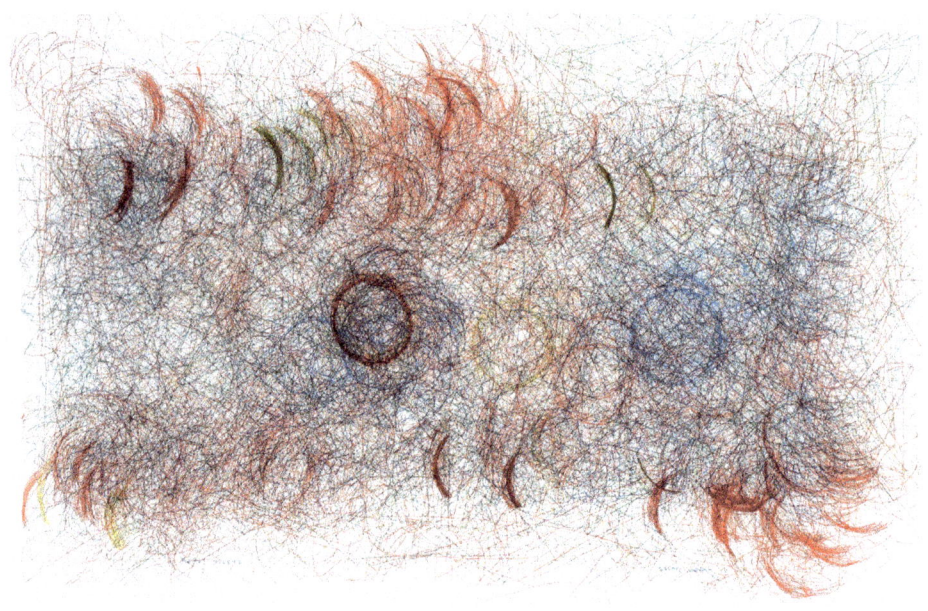

Fig. 6. Leonel Moura, *050517*, 2017, permanent ink on PVC canvas, 280 x 470 cm. Fondation Guy and Myriam Ullens Collection. Courtesy of the artist.

CHAPTER 5

Artists, Robots and 'Fun'

As proclaimed in the opening section, 'A Machine for Creating', in the catalogue for the exhibition *Artistes & Robots* at the Grand Palais in Paris in 2018, which focused on exploring multiple ways in which artists were using AI, 'The robots don't replace the artist or art: they invite us to ask what makes a work of art – and what makes an artist' (Dorléac and Neutres 2018, 59). That opening section provided an important historical overview of robotic art, or rather, of art co-produced with robots, since 1950. Many of the works included in the show were examples of painting or drawing robots: they were early predecessors of the 'painting like Rembrandt' trend, while being visually and technically complex artefacts in their own right. The exhibition opened with the striking cybernetic spatio-dynamic sculpture *CYSP 1* (1956), looking like a 3D Mondrian mobile, by the precursor of robotic art Nicolas Schöffer. Schöffer's pronouncement: 'The artist no longer creates work; he creates creation' (Neutres 2018, 189) could be taken as a motto for the show. The exhibition also featured a metallic reptile-like painting robot called *Méta-Matic no 6* by Jean Tinguely from

1959, and So Kanno and Takahiro Yamaguchi's *Senseless Drawing Bot*, a self-propelling machine placed on a skateboard and spraying graffiti-like squiggles on the wall. Then there was *Human Study #2.d, La Vanité* by Patrick Tresset: a stripped-down robotic arm holding a Bic pen, endlessly drawing a vanitas sketch on an old school desk while responding to human movement and gaze. Tackling the recurrent question about the nature of human and nonhuman creativity, the show's co-curator Jérôme Neutres has explained that artists working with robots, be it in their overtly machinic or more algorithmic form (or both), are creating machines that subsequently create works which those artists could not accomplish by themselves. Naturally, artists do not construct these machines just to get 'help' but rather to probe the limits of the human idea of creativity and of human-machinic assemblages. These works are thus described as collaborations between the artists and the robotic systems those artists have designed.

One of the most playful pieces in the exhibition was the aptly titled *Robot Art* by Leonel Moura, a 2017 iteration of his ensemble of small robotic vehicles traversing a large sheet of paper and leaving multicoloured line marks on it, to create a large abstraction. Moura explains that his robots have been equipped with environmental awareness and a small 'brain' that runs algorithms based on simple rules. The images obtained are not designed in advance but are rather the result of randomness and communication between the robots on the canvas (fig. 6). The artist's focus is on exploring complexity in art, especially as produced in collaboration with robots. It is worth quoting at length the exposition of Moura's ideas, presented in an interview with *Arts* journal in July 2018, as he articulated there very cogently many of the issues I am dealing with in this book, while also taking some steps towards outlining what I am calling a post-humanist art theory:

> It has been understood since at least the birth of abstraction that the main issue in art is neither its production nor the individual artistic sensibility by which it is guided. The main issue of art is art itself: its history, evolution, and innovative contributions. Anything can be considered art if validated by one of the several art world mechanisms including museums, galleries, specialised media, critics, curators, and/or collectors. Only in this way has the Duchampian ready-made and most of the art produced since been accepted and integrated into the formal art realm.
>
> Whether a work of art is made directly by a human artist or is the product of any other type of process is nowadays of no relevance. Recent art history shows many examples of art works based on random procedures, fortuitous explorations, *objets trouvés*, and arbitrary constructions. Surrealism, for example, even tried to take human consciousness out of the loop. More decisive is whether or not a new art form expands the field of art. Since the advent

of modernism, innovation has become a more important criterion in evaluating artistic projects than personal ability. ...

[S]ince robots like those I use are able to generate novelty, it must also be recognized that they have at least some degree of creativity. ... The algorithm and the basic rules introduced thereby via the robot microchip are not so very different, furthermore, from education. No one will claim that a given novel is the product of the author's school teacher. To the extent that the author, human or machine, incorporates new information, the art work becomes not only unique but also the result of the author's own creativity. In short, I teach the robots how to paint, but afterward, it is not my doing. (Moura 2018)

Moura's reflections implicitly engage with the dialogue on the nature of human and machine creativity initiated by Harold Cohen in 1973, when he launched his painting programme called AARON. Having raised the question of authorial singularity and distributed production of art in the computer science and media art communities, AARON has undergone multiple iterations since then, but it still demonstrates a rather narrow scope of creative possibilities when it comes to what and how it can paint. Moura seems to have taken things much further, visually and conceptually. Indeed, there is something playfully mischievous about his pronouncements cited above, especially as far as his supposed partial resignation from the role of the artist and his ceding of the creative ground to the machine and the algorithm are concerned. But it is only a very particular, and arguably old-fashioned and masculinist, idea of the artist as a creative genius at odds with the world, one who is also standing *above* the world, that is being challenged here. The robotic artist unveiled by Moura and his predecessors is *of the world*, he (or she, as the case may be in many current experiments with AI art) is also *in the world*. There is therefore a subtle socio-political message implied in this repositioning too. Apart from conceptual mischief, playfulness is actually what underpins many of the robotic art projects, both in their earlier and more recent guises. Many robots and other artefacts in the Paris exhibition were described as cute by the visitors. Their clunky movement, wobbly gait and unwieldy architecture often evoked a smile from members of the audience, who seemed mesmerised by the machines' picture-making efforts. It was not the images themselves that attracted attention but rather the whole performance of a machinic device attempting to draw or paint something, live. Art historian Laurence Bertrand Dorléac sees these 'joyful' painting machines as belonging in the tradition of performance art, surrealism, Dada and ludic experience (Dorléac 2018, 21-22). It is precisely the live, experiential aspect of robotic art rather than its machinic component that is highlighted as most significant for her.

Indeed, it could be argued that the 'joyfulness' of robotic and AI art is where its force lies, opening up the possibility of not only reaching to audiences outside the traditional exhibition spaces but also of redefining the very idea of what it means to make, display and distribute art. In this respect, the *Artistes & Robots* exhibition was still rather conventional: held in a white-walled cavernous exhibition space built in the Beaux-Arts style at the dawn of the twentieth century, it raised interesting questions about the potential of machinic creativity, while simultaneously inscribing robotic and AI art within the bounds of artistic grandeur and historical continuity. This was also a way of controlling its 'joyful' aspect by the high-brow mechanisms of architecture, culture and taste. In the meantime, the visually kitsch and derivative AI-inspired works of the 'style transfer' kind, which proliferate on the Internet, have embraced full-on the fun aspect of artistic production. Fabrice Bousteau, curator of another Paris exhibition devoted to digital and electronic art – *La Belle Vie numérique* held at Fondation Groupe EDF in 2017-2018 – has argued that digital and AI art opens up to, or even creates, different publics beyond traditional gallery goers precisely because it declares a wider realm of people as 'artists', from programmers and engineers through to Instagrammers (Lavrador 2017b, 9-11). It could therefore perhaps be suggested that AI has the potential to reboot what has been known, in a somewhat folksy way, as 'outsider art'. 'Style transfer' art is very much alive on the Internet, transforming the format of the museum and the gallery into a fluid display of experiment, joy and fun. But the conventional cultural institutions are also undergoing change with the arrival of new artistic and design practices. Neutres points out that 'Not only have the robots entered the museum, but they have actually even built it: the dome of the Louvre Abu Dhabi was designed by an algorithm' (2018, 11).

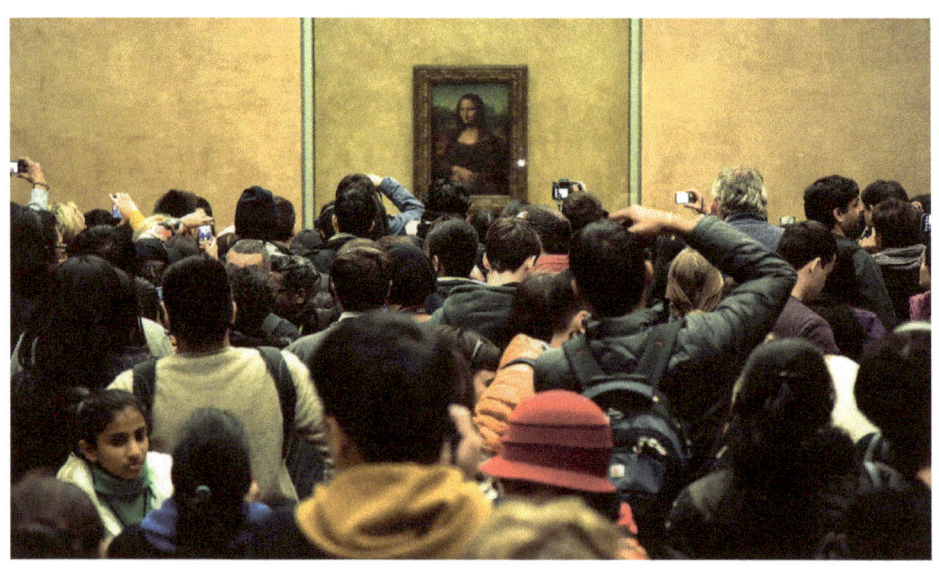

Fig. 7. Stephen R. Melling, *Mona Lisa*, The Louvre, 2014. Flickr, CC BY-ND 2.0.

CHAPTER 6

The Work of Art in the Age of Machinic Creation

AI-driven art can be understood as another turn in the entangled history of humans and technology. Challenging the notion of art as an expression of godlike creativity premised on the creation of absolute novelty *ex nihilo* (see Still and d'Inverno 2016), I want to suggest that art is always already emergent in- and with the world – and with the multiple technical apparatuses that shape the world. I am therefore inclined to take heed from psychologist Arthur Still and computer scientist Mark d'Inverno, who argue that AI research should remodel its concept of creativity along the lines of thought developed by philosopher of science A. N. Whitehead and premised on 'biological and social models of creativity'. For Whitehead, creativity is change that occurs in a way in which organisms act on their environments. Still and d'Inverno go on to claim that AI research would also benefit from adopting a concept of intelligence 'based on attentive inquiry' and arising out of the relations of the human with the environment. They end up with a proposal for an 'approach to designing systems supporting being in the world' (Still and d'Inverno 2016), which seems aligned with Moura's artistic ideas. Their framework is nonetheless still quite humanist, in that it gives precedence, although perhaps understandably, to *human* goals and *human* values as the driving force of future system design.[14] But it also creates an opening towards a more entangled and less antagonistic model of envisaging future AI systems, and hence towards a better AI discourse. The main premise of this discourse, I suggest, would not pitch the human *against* the machine but would rather adopt the human-with-the-machine, or even, more radically, the human-as-a-machine scenario, which we briefly explored earlier on.

Marcus du Satoy, a mathematician and author of *The Creativity Code: How AI Is Learning to Write, Paint and Think*, embraces multiple definitions of creativity engaged by AI researchers, including the pioneering work of Margaret Boden (2004), to suggest that being creative means diverging from the established path we carve out and then follow each day. He is particularly interested in Boden's idea of transformational creativity, which refers to those rare moments that become complete game changers. Those moments normally involve stepping outside the system, be it technological or cultural. 'That is where a machine might help', du Satoy suggests in a narrative twist that traces creativity *from* the machine *to* the human. '[P]erhaps it could give us that jolt, throw up a new suggestion, stop us from simply repeating the same algorithm each day. The machines might ultimately help us, as humans, to behave less like machines' (du Satoy 2019). Creativity in AI means for him a computer being able to 'come up with something new, surprising and of value' (2019), exceeding the pre-designed ideas of its coder. Computers could thus perhaps make us humans less computational. Interestingly, du Satoy points out that creativity 'meaning something novel with value is actually a very twentieth-century capitalist take on the word' (2019). This understanding of the term has its origin in the self-help books written in the 1940s by the advertising executive Alex Osborn, who attempted to implement innovation in businesses and their employees. The earlier meaning of creativity, offers du Satoy, referred to 'humans' attempts to understand being in the world' (2019). To suggest that creative activity, including art, has always been artificially intelligent, and that so have we, is thus not to engage in a form of intellectual acrobatics in which categories becomes fuzzy and everything starts looking like everything else. It is rather to trace the historical and philosophical legacy of the concept of creativity in the dominant narrative on AI today, with a view to recognising the false starts, failed promises and warped dreams that lie behind various narratives of technological innovation and progress.

In a poignant article titled 'YouTubers: The Last Artists', Polish writer Jacek Dukaj revisits Walter Benjamin's classic essay 'The Work of Art in the Age of Mechanical Reproduction' (1969) to consider what happens to the long-gone aura in art in the times of AI. For Benjamin the possibility of mechanically reproducing art works altered the original compact upon which art was premised by changing the artefacts from priceless objects of admiration to products that were part of the wider circulation of goods on the market. While acknowledging the loss of both the idea and the sensation of uniqueness in art prompted by this possibility of art's low-cost reproduction, the German philosopher identified a democratising potential in the latter process. The loss of the aura thus also went hand in hand with the rise in political awareness amongst those who had traditionally been excluded from the highbrow aesthetic experience, as their senses were now being drawn in to participate in the newly demystified circuit of artistic exchange. Benjamin's piece, first published in 1935, referred to the more traditional technologies of print, photography and film, while also offering a prescience of the wider cultural transformation that was going to occur in the digital age. Indeed, today almost all art and all cultural production can be digitised, allowing people to hold a Winged Victory of Samothrace, a Van Gogh or a Book of Kells in their hand, albeit flattened on a small glass rectangle. Dukaj also highlights the fact that AI is already involved in the production of the majority of cultural artefacts nowadays. For example, Hollywood blockbusters are edited on high-power computers using software with AI features that allow radical creative control after the shoot, but they are also planned, programmed and marketed on the basis of

Big Data obtained from user profiling across different platforms to check the product's desirability and minimise investors' risk. AI is here more than just a tool: it becomes an active agent in shaping tastes, regulating markets and defining what counts as mainstream visuality. The work of art is therefore not just mechanically reproduced but also algorithmically produced.

The current renewed interest in 'experiences' such as live concerts and immersive cinema does not contradict or even change the learned behaviours of the digital generation to have this supposed authenticity mediated – via Facebook, Twitter or Instagram. Indeed, the majority of people looking at the Mona Lisa in the Louvre today are actually photographing the experience of being in the crowd of people looking at the Mona Lisa (fig. 7). This is not to say that their encounter with the Mona Lisa is less 'authentic', although it is certainly less auratic in the Benjaminian sense. It is rather to point to the altered notion of authenticity in the age of the camera phone, encapsulated as it is by the Internet-age slogan: 'Pics or it didn't happen'. It may seem surprising that the so-called digital natives, brought up on image manipulation via Instagram filters or the in-phone alteration of features such as focus or depth of field, and the possibility of face-swap thanks to the implementation of AI algorithms, would usher in a call for such a seemingly retrograde guarantee. But the statement is premised on the evocation of the earlier function and magic of the image (see Benjamin 1969, Bazin 1960), coupled with its currently enhanced role as an affect-building device. Indeed, photographs increasingly function not as surfaces to be looked at and decoded but rather as digital gestures to be transmitted via email and social media, with a view to signalling affection, remembrance, call for attention or loneliness (see Frosh 2016). The visual retro-fetish which manifests itself in the repeated look of old film stock in digital images can perhaps be interpreted as a knowing embrace of authenticity *as a construct and figuration*, without relinquishing a desire for it. Instagram thus becomes a space in which one can attempt to resolve the ontological impossibility of eating a cupcake and having a cupcake.

Dukaj goes so far as to suggest that, in the times of AI, human life is the only auratic form of art left to us, especially the way it escapes the digital recording and preprogrammed behaviour. He is not talking here about some unmediated encounter between two humans outside the technological setup or evoking similar humanist fantasies. It is the YouTube stars, publicising their lives and the branded products that shape them, that are for him the last artists of today, turning lifestyle into an aesthetic experience while also externalising the knowledge about what it means to be human, and to behave like a human being, into the globally interconnected computer network. Gradually a new sense of 'being human' is therefore emerging, consisting of gestures, bodily movements, voice and language affectations, needs, desires and preferences drawn from the multiple data available online and then transmuted by the deep learning networks into what counts as 'the human experience'. But this is not a Black Mirror scenario in which avatars will look like us, generating a Bladerunner-like confusion over true human identity. Rather, the YouTube-generated sense of being human is premised on the recognition that, instead of positioning the human against the machine, AI exponentially amplifies the knowledge shared by marketing experts with regard to our desires and fantasies, while being much quicker and much more efficient at actualising them. We can therefore suggest that *AI dreams up the human outside the human*, anticipating both our desires and their fulfilment. For Dukaj, this state of events ultimately leads to a blind alley: a feeling of futility manifesting itself in 'a shrug, a dispirited grimace, a sense of lazy surprise in the face of absolute banality on offer' (2017). These sentiments represent for him 'the Homo sapiens artists' spirit in the times of AI'.

To sum up, I want to suggest that by raising these kinds of existential questions with regard to both human identity and purposeful human creative activity when confronted by AI, we perpetuate the idea of the human as an old-style cybernetic system – a system which, even if not humanist in the sense of being underpinned by concepts such as soul, spirit or unique human creativity, was just *adequately* homeostatic. In other words, pre-AI human in this model could both *be* an artist and *appreciate* art because there was just the right amount of material and data to process in order for something meaningful (for that human) to emerge.

However, once the information barrier has been crossed and all the possibilities for creation have supposedly been exhausted in advance, even if only on the virtual level, AI-driven art has become an ouroboros-like circle of random variations. This darker assessment of the current media landscape offers a rejoinder to ways of engaging with Internet-based AI art primarily in terms of 'fun', with disappointment, boredom and an impulsive yearning for one more click being fun's less glamorous counterparts. Human artists' and human publics' ennui in the face of AI as analysed by Dukaj could thus be interpreted as an excess of productivity: an outpouring of seemingly different outcomes whose structure has been predicted by the algorithmic logic that underpins them, even if not yet visualised or conceptualised by the carbon-based human. The pointless production of difference, whereby you may not be able to envisage or predict all the actual outcomes but where you can be sure of their pointlessness, is precisely where the biggest problem of a large section of what counts as AI-based art lies today. Indeed, it is not too much of an exaggeration to suggest that, its playful aspect aside, much of current AI art, especially of the computer- and data-based kind, ends up generating an odd combination of the fuzzy, the mindless and the bland. Thanks to its garish visibility, this version of AI art ends up serving as a PR campaign for corporate interests, dazzling viewers with the mathematical sublime of big data sets, rapid image flows and an intermittent flicker of light, sound and movement – with many arts organisations jumping on the AI bandwagon because this is where the promise of funding, excitement and innovation lies.

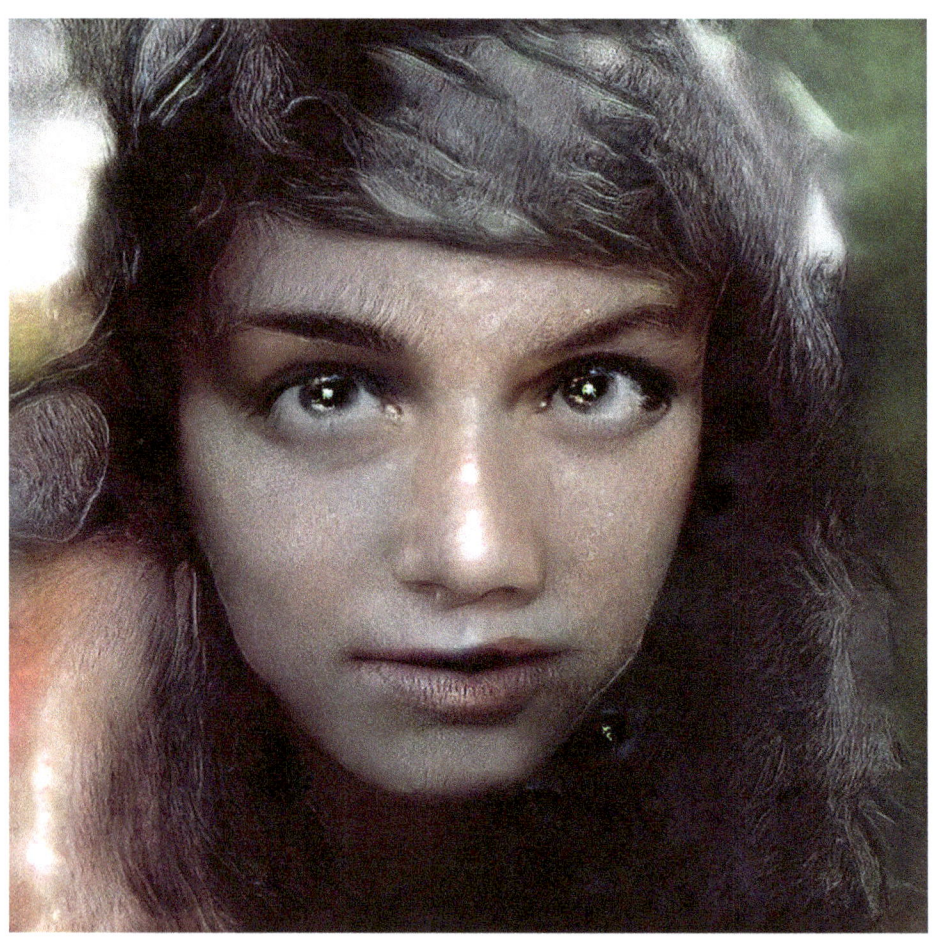

Fig. 8. Mike Tyka, from Work in progress: *Portraits of Imaginary People*, 2017, http://www.miketyka.com. Courtesy of the artist.

CHAPTER 7

Generative AI Art as Candy Crush

The 2017 edition of Ars Electronica took place under the banner of 'AI: Artificial Intelligence / Das Andere Ich'. In the catalogue accompanying the event, the Ars director Gerfried Stocker gushed in a tone that could have come straight from Silicon Valley investor publicity: 'the latest developments in artificial intelligence are truly astonishing, and they will soon be advancing exponentially. Never before has so much investment capital been [put] in pursuit of successful technologies and promising innovations' (Stocker 2017, 16). It is thus perhaps not accidental that much of the artistic research around AI is facilitated and sponsored by the main players within what has become known as platform capitalism: Google, Amazon, Facebook and Apple. Much of AI art is precisely platform art: generating visual and algorithmic variations within the enclosed system while teasing the public with the promise of novelty. Unlike most of the installation-based robotic art discussed earlier, this kind of AI art, described with the term 'generative', takes place across computer networks. Kindly put, much of generative AI art celebrates the technological novelty of computer vision, fast processing power and connection-making algorithms by regaling us with a dazzling spectacle of colours and contrasts as well as the sheer volume of data. Unkindly put, it becomes a glorified version of Candy Crush that seductively maims our bodies and brains into submission and acquiescence. Art that draws on deep learning and big data sets to get computers to do something supposedly interesting with images often ends up offering a mere psychedelic sea of squiggles, giggles and not very much in-between. It really is art as spectacle.

It is with this critical mindset, tinged with curiosity and fascination, that I approach much of the current work based on neural networks, code and algorithms by artists such as Gene Kogan, Mike Tyka, Memo Akten and Mario Klingemann. Kogan's *Neural Synthesis* was developed for the 'creativity exhibition' at NIPS (Neural Information Processing Systems) conference in 2017. The 2'41" video offers a psychedelic transmogrification of garishly multicoloured figures, faces and abstract patterns, slowly emerging before the viewer's eyes. Kogan's technique involves repeatedly optimising pixels in an image 'to achieve some desired state of activations in a convolutional neural network' (Kogan and lkkchung 2017) – i.e. a deep learning network, consisting of many layers of artificial neurons, which assumes the data it is being fed consists of images. That 'desired state' may end up looking like a dalmatian, a starfish or, indeed, a human face. The final layer in the network 'essentially makes a decision on what the image shows' (Mordvintsev 2015). An advanced version of this technique gained recognition in 2015, when Google released it to the public under the name of DeepDream (fig. 12). Put simply, DeepDream works by identifying and enhancing patterns in images, leading to the algorithm 'finding' human eyes or puppies in any regular photographs. The programme was originally developed 'to help scientists and engineers to see what a deep neural network is seeing when it is looking in a given image' but was quickly repurposed as a creative tool, which subsequently underwent various iterations. Works produced using the DeepDream algorithm were described with the term 'Inceptionism', 'which derives its name from the Network in network paper by Lin et al. [12] in conjunction with the famous "we need to go deeper" Internet meme' (Szegedy *et al.* 2014). Yet artists as well as the wider public quickly got bored with what a *Wired* journalist has described as 'Google's trippy neural network, which chews up reality and spits out slugs, dogs and eyes' (Temperton 2015).

A Google scientist called Mike Tyka, who was the author of some of the first large-scale artworks made with DeepDream, took some further steps with generative AI. His *Portraits of Imaginary People* (fig. 8), featured at Ars 2017 and produced by generative neural nets, are photorealistic yet also somewhat 'oil-painty' images of humans of different sexes, ethnicities and ages. To create them, the artist fed thousands of photos of faces from Flickr to a machine-learning programme called a generative adversarial network (GAN). GANs use two neural networks, where a neural network is basically an algorithm that is designed from bottom up, in a way that (supposedly) imitates the way the human brain works. The two neural networks in a GAN are placed in an adversarial relationship, with one tasked with generating convincing and correct input, the other – with controlling and improving upon this input, according to the truth/falsehood criteria. Their ongoing interaction makes both networks improve with time, learning from each other while trying to outdo each other in obtaining 'good' results. Requiring more knowledge of programming than the DeepDream interface did, GANs are now a frequent tool in the arsenal of many AI artists, especially those with science and engineering background. Given the source material used to train machine vision, it is perhaps unsurprising that canvas for such experiments is frequently provided by human faces. In a similar vein to Tyka's experiments, Memo Akten also explores human portraiture. His *Learning to See: Hello, World!* is a 'deep neural network opening its eyes for the first time, and trying to understand what it sees' (Akten 2017). This is a network that has not yet been fed anything. By being presented with a scanned image, via a surveillance camera, of a person standing in front of its computer host, the network attempts to figure out what it is seeing by identifying patterns in the information it has received. When faced with too much information, the network, like its human counterpart, also supposedly 'forgets'. As the artistic output, the human viewers are presented with a moving set of transmogrified, somewhat painterly faces.

But it is the work of Mario Klingemann – a self-proclaimed 'skeptic with a curious mind' working with neural networks, code and algorithms – that is worth looking at in more detail, partly due to the attention it has received but also because there is something really intriguing happening within (and around) his images. Another exhibitor at Ars Electronica 2017, he has also been an artist-in-residence at Google Arts & Culture: an online platform run by the Silicon Valley giant and featuring curated collections of artworks and other cultural artefacts. Klingemann's work builds on open source code written by engineers and shared with others who want to experiment with various AI applications, which he then tweaks for his own artistic purposes. Feeding large sets of data drawn from publicly available digital collections such as that of the British Library or the Internet Archive into a high-power computer, Klingemann aims to establish unusual encounters and connections between images and data points, while also visually rendering them in an interesting way – with the human artist ultimately deciding on this interestingness or its lack. His goal is 'to create algorithms that are able to surprise and to show almost autonomous creative behaviour' (Klingemann) with that sheepish 'almost' obscuring what is ultimately a largely mechanical process, although performed at a speed and intensity that exceeds that of any human reader of data. As a result, we get projects such as *Superficial Beauty*, featuring portraits that have been generated and enhanced by generative adversarial neural networks (GANs), or *Neural Face*, a collection of images of human faces scraped from various online repositories and programmed to 'evolve' into new faces. Using the neural network that provides biometric data for what looks like a human face, the artist trains the neural network in making *new* faces – which end up looking more photorealistic if he trains the network on photos, or more 'artistic' if he uses engravings or paintings as his training set. He also experiments with a less linear approach in that he not only derives faces from the face markers he feeds into the neural network but also derives face markers from pictures of faces and, finally, cross-feeds the data and the 'noise' between the two models to see what happens. Klingemann then combines the results obtained into videos showing multiple featureless faces seamlessly and dreamily morphing into one another (although with still relatively recognisable features of pretty white young girls), with an occasional exacerbation of a feature such the eye or the lip appearing slightly out of place.

Part Dali, part manga, part screensaver art, these rather kitsch images produced by the likes of Tyka, Kogan, Akten and Klingemann, especially in their moving variety, attempt to seduce viewers with a mildly fascinating transformation of humanist representationalism under the banner of 'uhm... what now?'. There is thus little difference, both aesthetically and in terms of creativity, between Google's DeepDream, which comes up with surreal images by finding and enhancing patterns between various data points, and what Klingemann terms 'cameraless neurophotography', which produces mesmerising yet somewhat creepy images made from parts of other images. Turning the mindless generation of images into an art form, the artist remains seemingly unaware that his art serves as a blanket for technical entrepreneurs' rather more pernicious, although not any less surreal, Deep Dreams. Yet, as Hito Steyerl argues in *Duty Free Art*, 'these entities are far from mere hallucinations. If they are dreams, those dreams can be interpreted as condensations or displacements of the current technological disposition. They reveal the networked operations of computational image creation, certain presets of machinic vision, its hardwired ideologies and preferences' (2017).

Indeed, generative art of this kind is premised on the banality of looking, with perception understood as visual consumption and art reduced to mild bemusement. It therefore does something more pernicious than merely introduce a new 'new aesthetic': slightly uncanny, already boring. '[H]ardwiring truly terrifying jargons of cutesy into the means of production', it enacts what Steyerl terms 'a version of corporate animism in which commodities are not only fetishes but morph into franchised chimeras' (Steyerl 2017). In projects of this kind, the artist's goals are clearly more aligned with the current developmental trajectories of corporately-funded AI, even if naturalised via the language of evolution. The language of evolution features prominently in the gen-art boys' discourse but theirs is a rather normative and linear idea of evolution understood as linear progression on an upward trajectory, not a process of false starts, zigzags and pointless repetitions. It thus fits perfectly with the technoevolutionary narrative of Silicon Valley 'visionaries' and investors, who are all sharpening their teeth at the next supposed technological leap. Through both their art and their discourse on art, Kogan, Tyka, Akten and Klingemann adopt a worryingly uncritical instrumentalism, where seemingly child-like curiosity is underpinned by the progressivist model of technological expansion towards some kind of improvement – of accuracy, data sets and, ultimately, art as we know it. They are thus poster boys for AI art as underwritten by Google in the way they incarnate the very ideas of progress, innovation and upward trajectory that drive the gung-ho progressivism of the AI 2.0 era. In their experiments that derive art from inputting data and noise into neural networks' feedback loops, they seem unwilling, and unable, to pursue any of the more serious questions raised by Steyerl in her indictment of computer vision art: 'Which faces appear on which screens, and why? ... Who is "signal," and who disposable "noise"?' (Steyerl 2017). Steyerl highlights the fundamentally political dimension of separating signal and noise in any kind of data set, with pattern recognition resonating 'with the wider question of political recognition' (2017).

Dreamy neural network art of this kind thus ultimately has a pacifying effect, anaesthetising us into the perception of banal sameness that creates an illusion of diversification without being able to account for *differences that matter* – for why and where they matter, when and to whom. It thus ends up enforcing a mode of existence that philosopher Franco 'Bifo' Berardi has called a 'neurototalitarianism'. Neurototalitarianism manifests itself in the utter intensification of semiotic (but we may also add, visual) simulation, in the end resulting in the sensation of panic in the social – and individual – neuro-system. 'In this condition of panic, reason becomes unable to master the flow of events or to process the semio-stimulations released into the Infosphere' (Berardi 2017). Would it be a step too far to state that AI art can actually be *mobilised*, wittingly or unwittingly, *in the service of* neurototalitarianism, using cutsey kittens and spaghetti with eyes to capture not just the attention but also the cognitive and neurological sphere of the modern political subject? This form of art enforces what Berardi has described as 'mental subsumption' (2017), whereby the automation of vision and of cognitive activity paves the way for the emergence of constantly stimulated yet passive subjectivity. It thus ultimately works in the service of neoliberalism, a mutated form of capitalism that, according to Byung-Chul Han, 'has discovered the psyche as a productive force'. Yet what gets produced here is 'mental optimisation' (Han 2017), for which Big Data, algorithms and AI serve as perfect conduits. Han calls this state of events a psychopolitics, which is his variation on Foucault's notion of biopolitics, whereby the subject mobilises technologies of the self not to create any forms of freedom but rather to succumb, 'willingly – and even passionately' (2017), to auto-exploitation (fig. 9). The brain, the mind, the eye, the heart, the finger, the tongue – the whole cortico-corporeal apparatus – all turn into a platform for the actualisation of this new form of psychopolitics, which drives 'the capitalism of "Like"' (Han 2017). Vision and perception are constantly stimulated in the process with the promise of a digital caress: they are being controlled by pleasure, rather than by coercion or prohibition, as was the case with Foucault's disciplinary model of society.

The self-quantification movement is one example where the self is constantly self-optimising, converting the principle of the care of the self into a form of labour but also into an aesthetic object in its own right. The process of self-optimisation is incessant, open-ended and always in danger of losing against someone with a higher score – yet it is also sustained by constant prompts of positivity: likes on Facebook or Instagram, pings from one's Fitbit, retweets. For Han, 'Neoliberal psychopolitics seduces the soul; it pre-empts it in lieu of opposing it. It carefully protocols desires, needs and wishes instead of "depatterning them"' (Han 2017). There is little difference in this model between AI art based on deep learning and neural nets, and the wider Internet aesthetics, with gifs, kittens and the constant flow of data on the Twitter stream or Facebook wall seeking 'to please and fulfil, not to repress' – but also being able to 'even read desires we do not know we harbour' (Han 2017). The Internet turns all of us into works of art, with our own self-aestheticisation via algorithms re-optimising our body and our prosthetic selves into a digital object of display: fully transparent, always on show. Han proposes 'idiotism', a withdrawal of communication and veiling oneself in silence, as the only salutary response to this state of events. Yet, rather than embrace this form of philosophical Luddism, I am more inspired by Berardi's call for the emergence of new cognitive abilities, or a new morpho-genesis he seeks. The idea here 'is to dismantle and reprogramme the meta-machine, creating a common consciousness and a common technical platform for the cognitive workers of the world' (Berardi 2017).

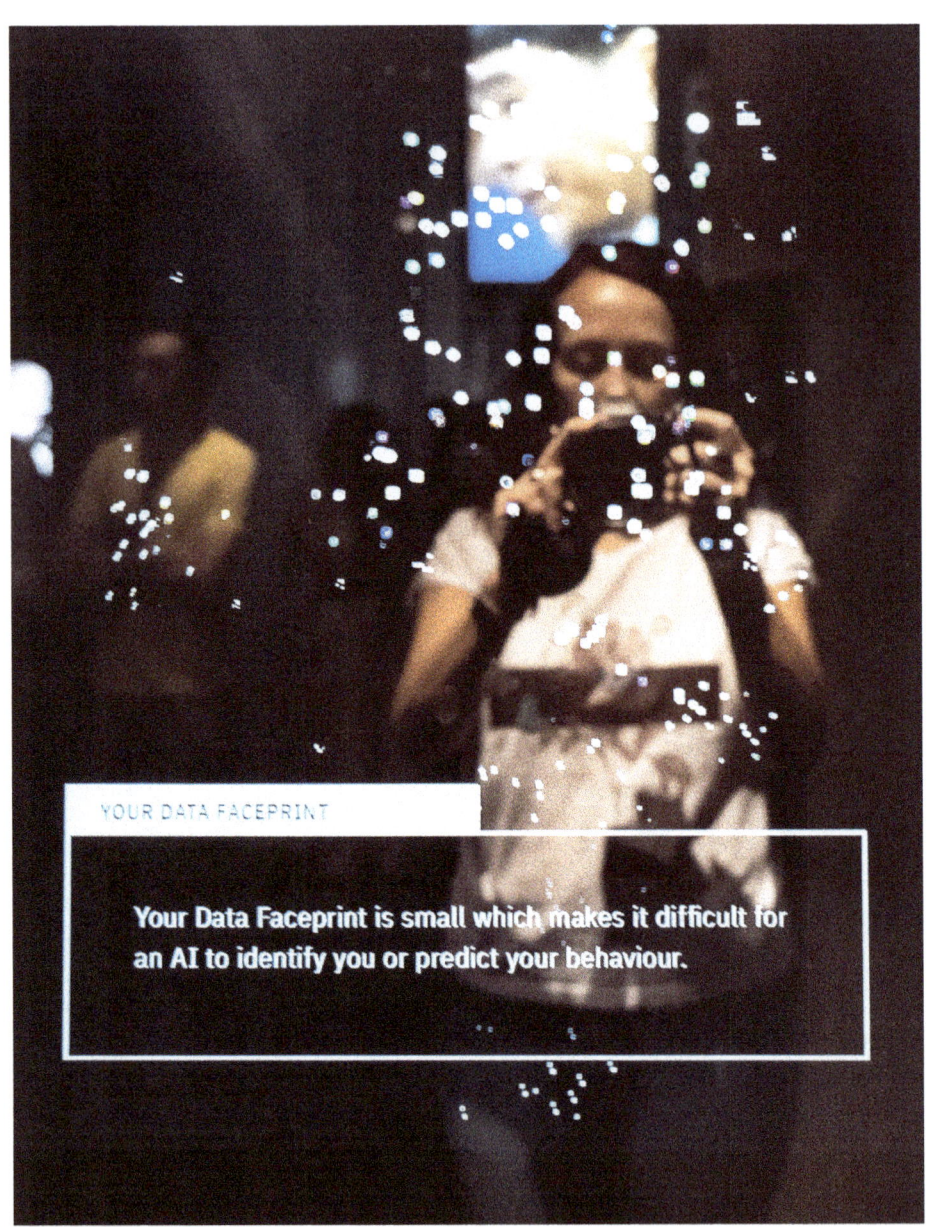

Fig. 9. Joanna Zylinska as (not) seen by the Data Faceprint identification algorithm developed by Nexus Studios, *AI: More Than Human*, Barbican Centre, June 2019.

Chapter 8

Seeing like a Machine, Telling like a Human

Artist Trevor Paglen's recent experiments with AI open up a different way of thinking about computation in relation to art and machine vision, while also revealing some limitations with regard to what art can and can't do. In his image-based practice Paglen has always interrogated how we see the world, focusing on the way in which the logic of total transparency promoted by the socio-political apparatus translates into global surveillance while also creating zones of opacity that hide the actual operations of power. And thus in *The Other Night Sky* (2010-11) he drew on data obtained from amateur satellite observers to track and photograph classified American satellites and space debris, in *Limit Telephotography* (2012) he used powerful telescopes to capture images of classified military bases, while in *Deep Web Dive* (2016) he photographed NSA-tapped underwater Internet cables at the bottom of the Atlantic. In all of those works the human-nonhuman assemblage was still driven by the human artist, who had mobilised the hybrid apparatus to reveal the limitations of human vision. Through this, Paglen raised questions about the inhumane aspects of some of the viewing practices installed by the current political regimes yet hidden from general view.

The problem of seeing has been very much of interest to the artist in his more recent work, which engages with AI technology. He frames his current approach as follows: 'Over the last ten years or so, powerful algorithms and artificial intelligence networks have enabled computers to "see" autonomously. What does it mean that "seeing" no longer requires a human "seer" in the loop?' (in Strecker non-dated). In an interview associated with his 2017 exhibition 'A Study of Invisible Images' at Metro Pictures in New York, Paglen highlights the fact that the majority of images produced today are not only generated automatically, without human intentionality or oversight, but are also intended for a nonhuman recipient: this or that section of the planetary computational system that Benjamin Bratton has deemed 'the stack' (Bratton 2016). The artist has in mind here photographs produced via face recognition technology which are increasingly used in policing, surveillance and access; computer vision directing the self-driving cars; or cameras on drones used to allow algorithm-driven 'killer robots' to determine worthy targets.

Paglen's project *It Began as a Military Experiment* (2017) included in the Metro exhibition features rows of colour portrait photographs, showing seemingly regular subjects of different genders, ethnicities and ages – with the display looking like an updated version of August

Sander's *People of the 20th Century*. Only a very close look allows the viewer to detect grid-like white symbols, which have been superimposed on the subjects' faces. From the accompanying materials we learn that the photos had been drawn from the so-called FERET database containing thousands of photos of people – many of them workers at a military base in Maryland – which had been collected on behest of DARPA (the Defense Advanced Research Projects Agency) to help develop facial recognition technology. To advance the technology, the military needed to train algorithms in correct pattern recognition by feeding the network thousands of similar faces and teaching it to recognise variations between them. Paglen spent months going through the FERET database to select individual images, which he subsequently retouched and colour-corrected, and then ran them through an algorithm to identify key points in the faces. '[T]these photos represent some of the original faces of facial recognition – the "Adams and Eves" that nearly all subsequent facial recognition research has been built upon' (in Strecker non-dated). In this sense, they not only hint at Sander's totalising humanism but also reference Edward Steichen's *Family of Man* photographic exhibition held at MoMA in 1955, whose ambition was to reveal a supposed universality of human experience while also promoting a soft version of US imperialism. And yet a strange shift occurs in this presumed Adamism – a term Roland Barthes used ironically in *Mythologies* to refer not just to the presupposed originary unity of 'all men' in Steichen's exhibition that the FERET database perpetuates, but also to a 'lyricism' which immobilises humans in their place by making their social condition look eternal (Barthes 1973, 102). What is new about the FERET images is that they are not aimed at human eyes: as a training set for a facial recognition algorithm, their goal is to establish this commonality-in-difference for machine vision. Indeed, these images are not meant to be seen at all by humans but are rather going inside the black box that AI has become. The fact that most AI research has been funded by the military, with DARPA, the original funders of Internet development, also sponsoring 'more AI research than private corporations and any other branch of the government' (Barrat 2013, 180) from the 1960s through to the 1990s, means that AI is literally a military project, even if developed by external companies and research universities. It is precisely the impossibility of knowing what is *in* the database – not only due to the lack of access but also due to the sheer physical impossibility on the part of humans to sift through all the data – that drives Paglen's current work.

This black-boxing of AI technology hides, for example, the data bias of human engineers who construct the supposedly universal data sets. As Alexander Strecker, editor of *LensCulture*, wrote in his review of Paglen's exhibition: 'imagine the first time a self-driving car has to choose between two children who have run out into the road, one white and one black. If the computer "sees" the black child as a small animal, due to the bias of the training sets it has been given, its choice will be clear' (Strecker non-dated). Yet it is not only the question of data bias – which some AI researchers argue can be overcome by feeding the system a wider set of data, training people in labelling the data better, making them undergo bias awareness training or simply paying them more – that emerges as a concern here. A deeper problem lies in the very idea of organising the world according to supposedly representative data sets and having decisions made on their basis, in advance and supposedly objectively. Such technologies are of course already in use: we can mention here not only face recognition at border control and other security access points, but also Facebook photo tagging algorithms, identification of bank cheque deposits or rapid decisions about credit. One might even go so far as to argue that what we humans perceive as ethical decisions are first and foremost corporal reactions, executed by an 'algorithm' of DNA, hormones and other chemicals that push the body to act in a certain way, rather than outcomes of a process of ethical deliberation concerning the concept of good and the value of human life. As mentioned earlier, I am therefore reluctant to analyse AI developments by pitching the human against the machine in order to wonder whether 'they' are going to get 'us' or not. But I do want to throw some light on the very debate on AI by shifting from a polarised and dualist narrative to one that interrogates entangled human-nonhuman agency while also raising political questions. Technologically-aware art can create a space for interrogating who funds, trains and owns our algorithms. This interrogation is important because, as shown by Safiya Noble in *Algorithms of Oppression: How Search Engines Reinforce Racism*, 'data and computing have become so profoundly their own "truth" that even in the face of evidence, the public still struggles to hold tech companies accountable for the products and errors of their ways. These errors increasingly lead to racial and gender profiling, misrepresentation, and even economic redlining' (Noble 2018). Critical projects such as those by Paglen encourage us to ask: Whose vision is AI promoting? Who is doing the looking, in what way and to what purpose?[15]

Paglen's project *Sight Machine* (2017) was aimed at exploring precisely these questions. A collaboration with Kronos Quartet and light installation company Obscura Digital, it involved staging a concert in a San Francisco warehouse, accompanied by the projections of various bits of data driven by AI algorithms. As well as displaying, in frequent motion, one of the face recognition training data sets discussed above, the artist had installed a number of cameras in the warehouse, with feeds going into the video mixer and the hardware. The cameras then made visible on the screen behind the band renderings of outlines of the human members of the band in the form of multicoloured squiggles, circles and squares. The artist and his team occasionally turned the camera on the audience to allow them to see themselves being seen by the computers, with their faces identified as faces and also rendered as rectangles. The idea behind the project was to examine the architecture of different computer vision systems by trying to learn what it was that they were seeing. Yet we should ask to what extent this is actually still 'seeing'. And are we still talking about intelligence? Or are they just behaviours that *look like* seeing and intelligence to us, their human interpreters?

Echoing a quip that is popular with AI researchers, 'Can the submarine swim?', these questions are important because the systems put in motion that enable computer vision and other forms of AI determine who and what is allowed in and what isn't. Much translation work had been involved in Paglen's *Sight Machine*, but at the end of the day the performance revealed the basic untranslatability of data between different recipients, resulting from the opacity of code (from brute force algorithms of the 1960s systems to contemporary deep learning frameworks such as TensorFlow, Torch and Caffe). It is precisely in that very gesture of attempting to undertake the work of translation that the incompatibility between different cognitive frameworks and different forms in which intelligence is embodied was revealed. The project thus succeeded and failed at the same time: it failed at transparency, at revealing (to us) what and how computers supposedly see, but it succeeded at unveiling this translation gap – which is also an epistemological and ontological gap. Paglen himself recognised as much in the essay co-written with AI researcher Kate Crawford, when they posed a seemingly rhetorical question: 'What if the challenge of getting computers to "describe what they see" will always be a problem?' (2019). And even though Paglen's project failed the classic Marxian promise that revealing the conditions of injustice would lead to increased political activity and eventual liberation, that promise itself has been debunked by the public responses to platform capitalism. It would be naïve to think that people are unaware that, for example, Amazon is spying on them, that Google tracks their every move or that Facebook mines their personal data for commercial gain, yet the percentage of those who permanently sign off social media or remove their personal data from the cloud is – and indeed *can* be – very slim. Yet what Paglen unveils is precisely the fact that vision itself is changing and that we cannot ever truly see the conditions of our material existence. He also shows us that a new network of visibility, much of which remains permanently obscured from human vision, has now emerged which has the potential to redefine radically what counts as visible and what doesn't – or *what counts, full stop.*

We could therefore conclude that Paglen's work reveals the impossibility of 'seeing it all' on the part of the human, while also demonstrating how the link between seeing and knowing has been ultimately severed in the algorithmic culture that organises our social and political lives. And yet, as with his previous projects, there is something romantically futile about this artistic gesture, premised as it is on unveiling the dark machinations of 'the stack'. To say this is not to dismiss his artistic undertakings but rather to suggest that the success of Paglen's work lies in its parergonal nature: to really 'get' what he is showing we need to engage not just with the images he produces but also with the narrative about machine vision, the human intervention into the limits of the image and the discourse about art making. The term *parergon*, referring to a supplementary remark, additional material or ornament whose function is merely to embellish the main work (i.e. the *ergon*), has been immortalised in art theory by Jacques Derrida. In his reading of Kant's *Critique of Judgement* included in *The Truth in Painting*, Derrida takes issue with the idea of a self-contained nature of the work of art, conveyed by the belief in its supposed intrinsic value and beauty, by literally bringing the work's framing into the picture. 'A parergon comes against, beside, and in addition to the ergon, the work done [*fait*], the fact [*le fait*], the work, but it does not fall to one side, it touches and cooperates within the operation, from a certain outside. Neither simply outside nor simply inside' (Derrida 1987, 54). The supposedly secondary function of the framing, be it literal or conceptual, is argued to be actually foundational to the artwork's existence and recognition as an artwork, as its very existence delineates and preserves the artwork's identity. For Derrida, a work of art is therefore never self-contained, it always depends on its parerga – frames, ornaments, commentaries – if it is to be recognised in its proclaimed uniqueness and singularity. And thus to say that Paglen's work is parergonal is not to criticise it for its presumed lack but rather to acknowledge its (perhaps knowing) reliance on the grid, the network and the cloud. In other words, Paglen's projects about seeing machines mobilise human intelligence and machinic technology to say and show us something, while also revealing our own cognitive and political limits and blind spots. His practice does not amount to producing political art *per se*, but it does engage our sense *and* sensibility to reprogram the human cognitive-sensory apparatus – and maybe to open it up to a different hack.

This kind of approach inscribes itself in the postconceptual mode of artistic production, in that it is still driven by concepts, but it is also very much reliant on their material enactments and visualisations. Interestingly, in Paglen's case these enactments and visualisations *fail by design*. This is to say, they fail on the level of actually showing us anything meaningful – but this is because their role is not illustrative bur rather allegorical.[16] Paglen's works thus serve as parables, revealing a hidden story, with a deeper moral meaning, beyond what's on show. Tim Clark has described the artist as 'one of the most urgent chroniclers of our times, highlighting the forces that lay beyond what is immediately evident' (2019). This allegorical method of working is mobilised not just in the projects discussed above but also in Paglen's exhibition *From 'Apple' to 'Anomaly'* (2019-2020), staged at the Barbican Centre's The Curve. For the show the artist had printed out some 30,000 photographs from ImageNet, the largest and best-known dataset which is widely used to train computers in how humans see and recognise images. He then installed the square prints in a mosaic-like fashion, by following aesthetic and associative cues: from (Magritte's) apple to anomaly. The final result was a huge colourful tapestry which offered a visual journey through the clouds of images and concepts, while also producing a sensory overload in the viewers (or rather *walkers*, because the project required an active traversal of the gallery space alongside the exhibition wall to be able to take it all in, and this taking in could only occur in sections due to the curved, corridor-like shape of the space). Contrary to the promises of the wall text, the work did not so much expose the algorithmic bias of the online databases used to construct AI training sets, or even reveal those databases' impossibly large size. But what it did do was send out a moral alert to visitors about the transformation of vision that was taking place in the wider world. *From 'Apple' to 'Anomaly'* can thus be positioned as one of the seeing machines analysed elsewhere by the artist – not because it sees anything *by itself* or even approximates the way machines see, but rather because 'machines become autonomous systems that intervene and are coercive in the world' (Clark 2019). It thus symbolises a larger infrastructure of perception and cognition which is currently being constructed at different scales – and which, arguably, will soon change our ways of being in the world, as individuals and as citizens.

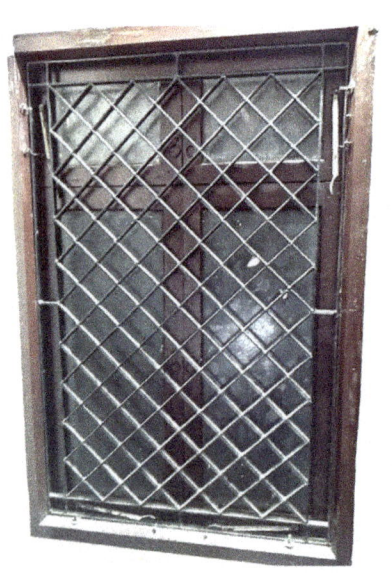 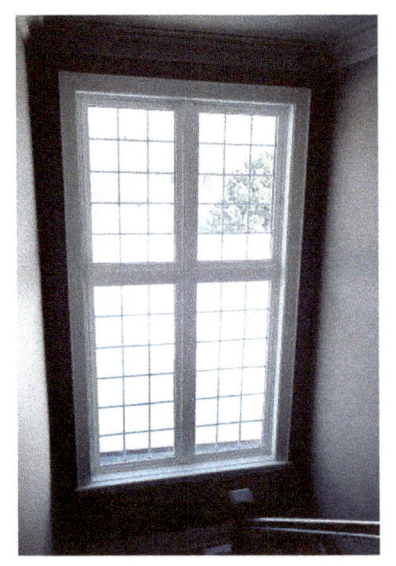

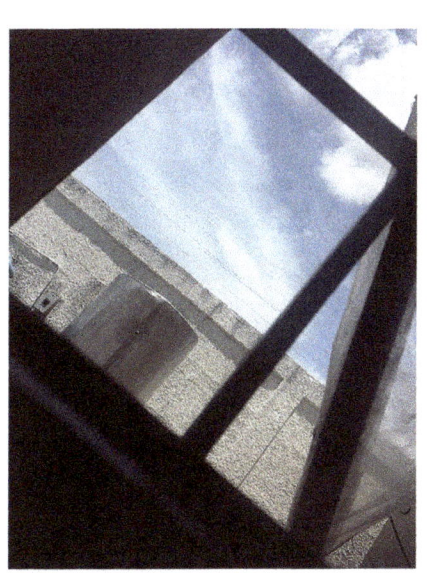
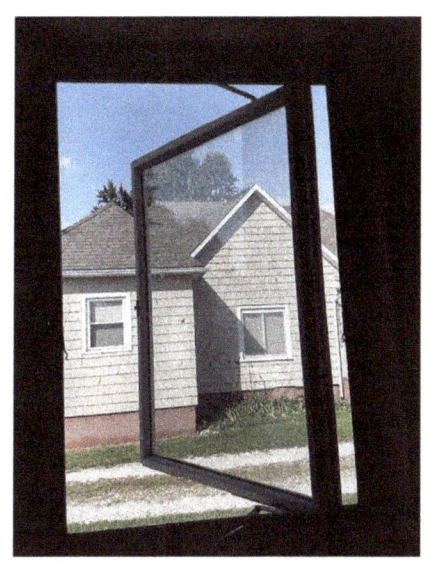

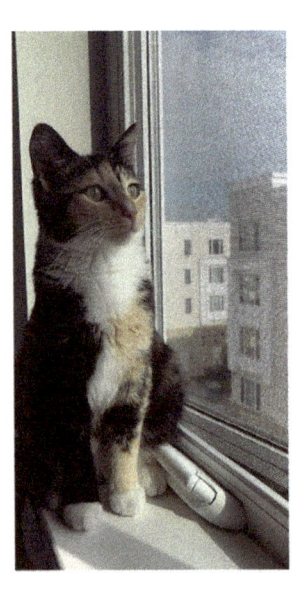 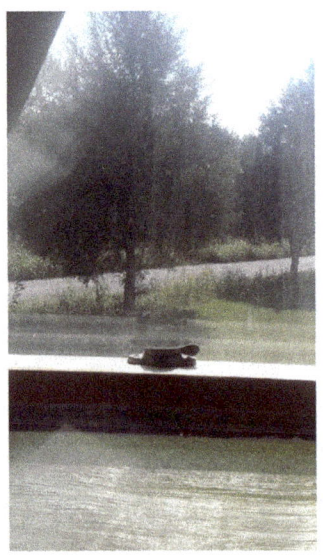

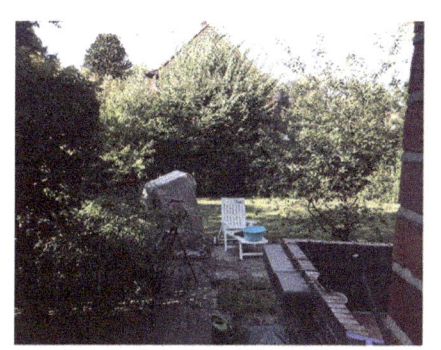
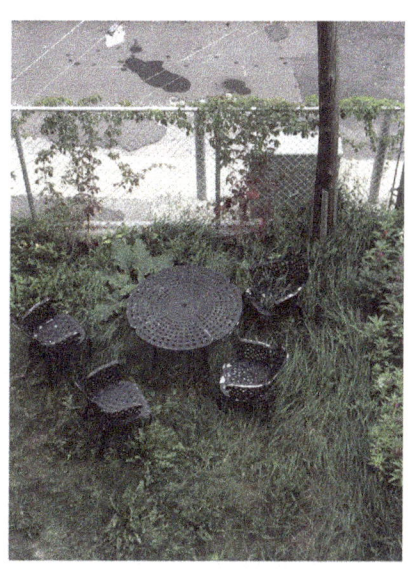

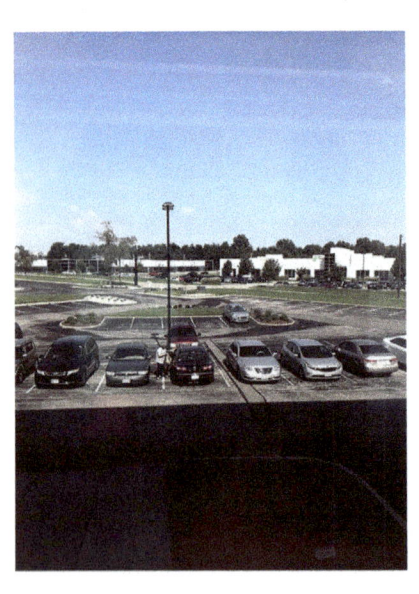 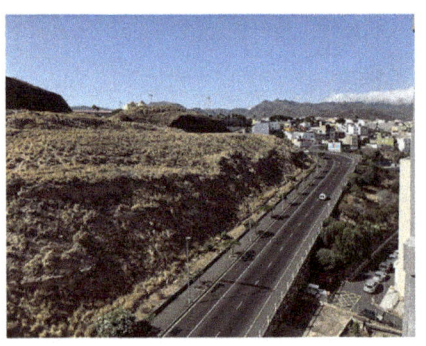

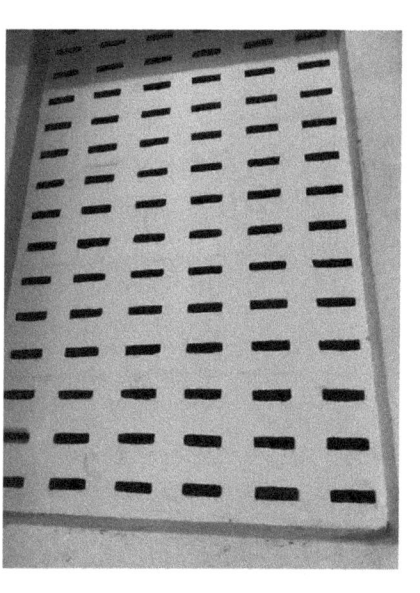
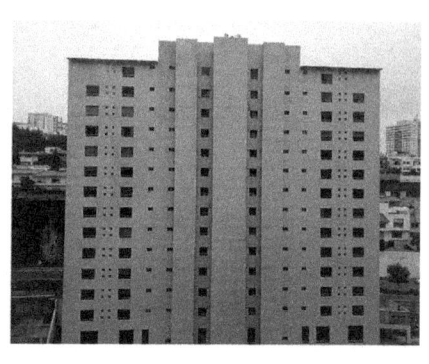

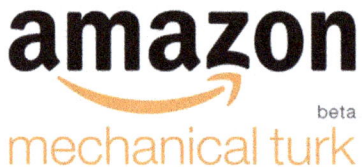

Total HIT value: $35

Figs. 10a-10f. Joanna Zylinska, excerpts from *View from the Window*, 2018. The complete project can be seen by scanning the QR code below or visiting: https://vimeo.com/344979151

CHAPTER 9

Undigital Photography

The notion of 'seeing machines' referenced in the previous chapter is actually a term used by Trevor Paglen to describe the contemporary condition of photography. In a series of blog posts written for Fotomuseum Winterthur in 2014, Paglen proposed an expanded understanding of the photographic medium, encompassing 'the myriad ways that not only humans use technology to "see" the world, but the ways machines see the world for other machines' (Paglen 2014). His definition includes various image-capture apparatuses, from mobile phones through to satellite cameras, but it also incorporates data, storage systems, interpretation algorithms and, last but not least, the technologies of perception that emerge as part of the networked photographic practices – and that establish and legitimate particular regimes of visibility. Most importantly, the concept of photography-as-seeing-machines highlights the fact that to focus 'too closely on individual images is entirely to miss the point' (Paglen 2014). With this argument Paglen offers a blow to the art-historical understanding of photography in terms of singular historical records and framed artefacts. It is not even that digital technology has resulted in the supposed overproduction of images today, with singular photographs giving way to image and data flows. It is rather that photographs cannot be treated as discrete entities because they are part of the wider technological network of production and perception: the are both objects to be looked at and vision-shaping technologies, for humans *and* machines. Their identity as discrete images is thus performatively established by the very acts of looking at them – but we must bear in mind that the 'looker' is not always human.

There is an affinity between Paglen's conceptualisation of photography in terms of 'seeing machines' and my own notion of 'nonhuman photography', developed in the book of the same title (Zylinska, 2017). The book's argument was premised on my conviction about the inadequacy of the traditional photography theory for analysing the image landscape today, because, as Paglen points out, 'Susan Sontag's seminal work has little to say about the infrared imaging system on a Reaper drone' while 'applying Roland Barthes' ideas to the billions of images in London's city-wide surveillance archives would be utterly absurd' (2014). For me, the concept of 'nonhuman photography' refers to photographs that are not *of, by* or *for* the human (see Zylinska 2017, 5), encompassing images as diverse as depopulated vistas, satellite pictures and QR codes. Even though the opening premise of *Nonhuman Photography* is that today, in the age of CCTV, drone media, medical body scans and satellite imaging, photography has become increasingly decoupled from human agency and human vision, I have also suggested that even those images that have been taken by the human entail a nonhuman element. This element, executed by means of technical and cultural algorithms, is revealed by the fact that most people's wedding photographs, holiday snapshot and Instagram feeds look uncannily similar.

The recognition of this cultural iterability allowed me to suggest, as I have earlier on here, that humans have always been technological, i.e. that we have run on algorithms – from DNA to behavioural instructions developed in various cultures to legitimate and promote certain ways of doing things over others. If we accept this premise, we will then have to conclude that all manifestations of art, and specifically all images, starting from cave paintings, have depended on bodily prostheses, cognitive extensions and expanded modes of intelligence. My concept of 'nonhuman photography' thus arguably goes further (or deeper) than Paglen's idea of 'seeing machines' because it not only studies *humans as seen by machines* or *machines that see things outside the human spectrum*, but also because *it understands humans as (non-Cartesian, embodied and entangled) seeing machines*. Last but not least, it also reaches towards the geological past, with the universe positioned as a giant camera making photoimagistic impressions on a variety of surfaces, from rocks through to skin.

Yet, rather than enter into terminological competition with Paglen, whose work I greatly admire, I am more interested in bringing his theory of machinic sight into a conversation with my own work that probes the algorithmic aspect of perception and vision across apparatuses, species and time scales. The rationale for this conversation is an attempt on my part to imagine better ways of seeing the world at a time when it is being reshaped by the discourses and practices of AI. It is also to envisage better ways of acting in the world. While I acknowledge that both seeing and acting will be undertaken by human and nonhuman agents, the reflective process on what constitutes this goodness and what forms it may take, and also on the competing claims to its validity – depending on one's political and ontological constitution – will be uniquely human. To enact this encounter, I want to offer a new conceptual figuration: 'undigital photography'. The term is not fully mine: I have borrowed it from the academic discipline of Computational Photography, a field which deals with images captured and processed by means of digital computation rather than as a result of optical processes. 'Undigital photography' is the alternative moniker given to this new field in which 'the snap is only the start' (Kelion 2013) and where changes to focus, lighting, framing or depth of field can take place *after* an image has been taken. It goes without saying that computation has been part of mechanical image making for a long time now: we can think here of Photoshop or internal processing of jpg or even raw files by various digital cameras. What changes with computational photography is the *inherent* instability of the outcome of the imaging process, with its openness to manipulation constituting the very ontology of the undigital image – and not just a possibility aimed at professionals or advanced amateurs, like it was with more traditional digital images produced by early mobile phone or DSLR cameras. Yet in the term 'undigital photography' I also see a conceptual and poetic promise for rethinking our current frameworks and modes of understanding image making as developed in both media theory and visual culture. The term thus offers new possibilities for thinking photographically in the age of AI. This terminological reinscription is made partly in jest: as promised earlier, I aim to cut through the smoke and mirrors that envelop the discourses of computation and AI. But I also want to raise broader questions about the conditions of image making, creativity and labour today.

Undigital photography recognises the (human) history of photography: its artistic legacy, affective attachments and technological residues. But it repositions this history as premised on events enacted by human agents along the lines of technical assemblages – assemblages which *also* include humans. This repositioning is undertaken with a view to offering a more complex understanding of the relations of causality, influence and change, but also of human responsibility and the possibilities of its enactment as part of such assemblages. It is an attempt to respond to Flusser's probing question as to what humans can do in a universe driven by geophysical forces which are not of our making (see Flusser 2011, 16-19) – and to explore what

Chapter 9

forms human creativity can take, be it on an artistic, engineering or political level. This attempt also entails questioning to what extent such creativity can ever be *solely* human. The renewed interest in, and research into, AI makes such an enquiry ever more urgent.

As well as constituting the key theme of this book, my contribution to this enquiry has taken the form of an (un)photographic project that has engaged with 'artificial artificial intelligence'. The latter term is what Amazon has been informally calling its Mechanical Turk (MTurk) platform, an online 'marketplace' connecting labour suppliers with providers worldwide. The 'labour' here consists of HITs, 'human intelligence tasks' usually involving simple mechanical actions performed on digital data, such as tagging photographs or filling in surveys, priced very cheaply (from 0.01 to 0.25 cents per task on average). The project basically puts humans in the role of machines, as it would be too impractical and costly to program a computer which could perform such tasks.

MTurk's collective force has actually played a significant if somewhat obscured role in the history of machine (aka deep) learning and AI, especially as far as image recognition and machine vision are concerned. The 14-milion-item database of photographs called ImageNet, which Pagen's project *From 'Apple' to 'Anomaly'* discussed in the previous chapter explores, only really took off as a convincing and efficient collection of training sets after the engagement of MTurk labour. ImageNet began its life as a relatively small database of 10,000 labelled images of various objects, divided into twenty classes. It was launched in a modest poster presentation in 2009.[17] Those images were aimed at training computers to recognise similar objects on their basis. Yet ImageNet needed a much wider set of images to be effective. Once social media took off, computer scientists under the guidance of Stanford University's Fei-Fei Li took the project further by being able to benefit from the wide availability of 'free' photos across various platforms. However, even though they managed to scrape off millions of images from the Internet, they were still presented with the difficulty of having to label such a huge data set. It was the hiring of the globally distributed army of 50,000 anonymous MTurkers in 2007 that allowed them to accomplish this mammoth task, a task which could not have been undertaken by even the most efficient research team at any one institution. In time ImageNet became the leading training set for computer vision. Yet these developments in computer vision have been premised on obscuring, to a large extent, the human and machinic infrastructures that assisted its development, with their mutable energy flows and unacknowledged perceptive and epistemological blind spots.[18] MTurkers' labour thus became part of ImageNet's 'black box'.

In my own project, undertaken as part of the research for this book, I was not so much interested in opening up the black box of the nascent AI technology as in peering inside the invisible enclosure that housed the MTurk labour force, which assisted its emergence. I thus commissioned 100 MTurkers to take one photo of a view from a window of the room they were in at the time (figs. 10a-10f). The instructions clearly stipulated that if there was no window in the room, they should go to the next available room with a window and take a photo from there. They were also asked not to upload stock photos, existing images from the web or their old photos. I explained that this HIT was for a research/art project which studied human and machinic creativity. The participants were asked to make their photo look beautiful, according to their own idea of what this meant. Postprocessing was allowed but not required. The HIT was priced at double the US living wage (per hour), which probably explains why all the tasks had been snapped up and fulfilled almost immediately – although, given that the task was to take 1-2 minutes on average (precisely because I wanted a somewhat automatic production of the scene, to be executed by time-poor humans in assembly with their heavily automated phone cameras), I could hardly be said to be alleviating world poverty.[19] Indeed, the very act of using MTurk for this project was not unproblematic, as I will show further on, and could actually be seen to be perpetuating unfair labour conditions worldwide by validating Amazon's platform. The exploration of these issues and conditions also formed the fabric of my project.

I do not know where the MTurkers that responded to my call came from, although it is possible to make some guesses from the images themselves, using signage, architecture and vegetation. According to a 2018 study, 'Most of the [MTurk] workers are from the USA (75%), with India (16%) being second, followed by Canada (1.1%), Great Britain (0.7%), Philippines (0.35%), and Germany (0.27%)' (Difallah *et al.* 2018, 3). The composition of a group of available workers at any one time also depends on what time it is in different time zones. The geographical concentration of the platform's workers is unsurprising given that, even though many of the advertised tasks are very simple, they require a command of the English language to understand and perform them, which puts native and near-native speakers at an advantage. Yet MTurkers operate anonymously and are only identified through their assigned number, creating an illusion of a fluid mobile labour force that forms part of the digital cloud.

The idea behind my project was to rematerialise the cloudy vapour behind this narrative by creating a group portrait of MTurkers' locations. Neither conventional portraiture nor landscape photography, the collective image-base of *View from the Window* offers instead a non-comprehensive demographic snapshot of the global workforce, looking out. The concept and the title entail a return to the mythical 'first photo' in the history of photography: Joseph Nicéphore Niépce's *View from the Window at Le Gras* (1826 or 1827). Due to the limited sensitivity of photographic materials – namely, the pewter plate covered with bitumen – at the time, Niépce's image of a view from a window of his country house in Bourgogne took eight hours to expose. It resulted in 'a scene which the human eye could never see', with sunlight and shadow being visible on two sides of the buildings at left and right (see Anthes in Modrak 2011, 112). I argued elsewhere that the first image in the history of photography therefore presented a distinctly nonhuman vision (Zylinska 2017, 21-22), while also enacting a nonhuman agency at the heart of its production. It is also for this reason that I chose Niépce's image as a conceptual frame for my MTurk project. The 'artificial artificial intelligence' of Amazon's invisible and distributed labour force can therefore be described as 'undigital' in the sense that, even though it uses digital technology to perform at least partially digital tasks, simulating the work of machines in its quiet efficiency, it also ruptures the seamless narrative and visualisation of the machine world. It does this by bringing the material traces of human bodies and their locations into the picture, literally. The view from the window also shows us that *there is a window* in the first place (or not). This window takes on the form of a metal or wooden frame holding a glass pane (and, occasionally, curtains, shutters or a mosquito net) that brings in the outside world. It simultaneously keeps this outside world at bay, precisely as 'the outside', the place where the person looking out *is not*. Yet the window here also stands for the rectangular visualisation of the software interface patented by Microsoft and used by other operating systems as part of their user-friendly GUI – and, last but not least, for the computer screen behind which the MTurk workers sit, interfacing with the network that hires them. The MTurk labour force is therefore collectively framed by multiple nested windows, which both hold them together and keep them apart.

In her book provocatively titled book, *Artificial Unintelligence*, which deals with a misguided belief that computation can solve all complex social issues (see Broussard 2018, 11), Meredith Broussard argues that 'How you define AI depends on what you want to believe about the future' (89). Yet, unlike Broussard's effort to humanise technology and bring the human back to the centre of the technological assembly, *View from the Window* aims to do something different. Indeed, for me such a well-meaning effort at humanisation can only ever be misguided because it is premised on severing the human's constitutive relationship with technology. What the project does offer though is a different vantage point for perceiving this relationship at this particular moment in time – and, more importantly, a recognition *that there is a vantage point*, and that the 'view from nowhere' (see Haraway 1998) promoted by most AI designers ends up putting a very specific (white, male, ahistorical) human in the picture. *View from the Window* thus also suggests that, as well as break through the glass ceiling, (un)digital workers may be ready to start smashing their virtual windows at any time. How is that for the 'AI breakout' many AI researchers are scared of?

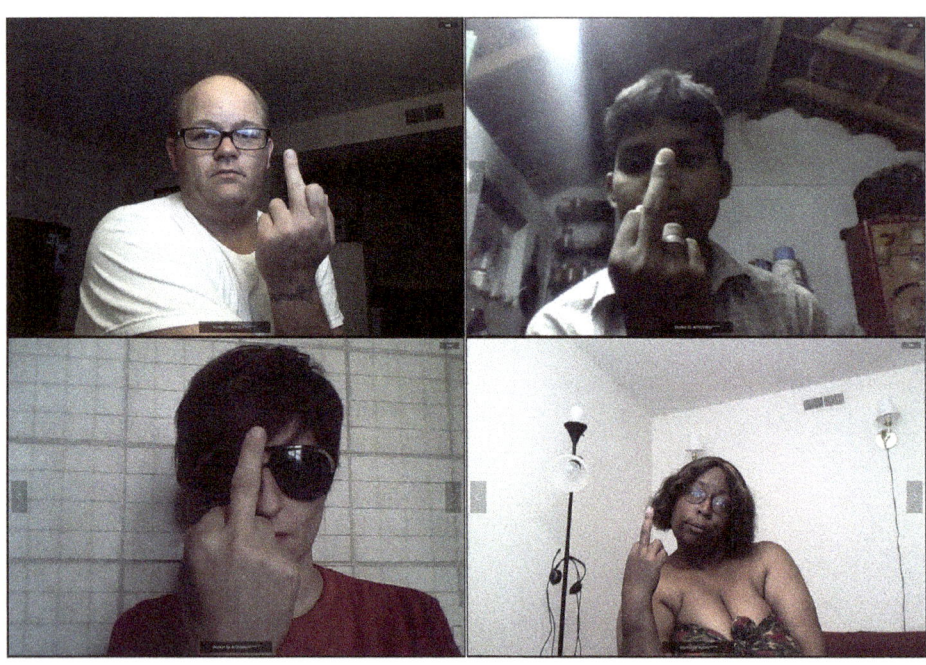

Fig. 11. Guido Segni, four images from *The Middle Finger Response (Crowd workers of the world, united in a gesture)*, 2013. Courtesy of the artist.

CHAPTER 10

An Uber for Art?

C omputer scientists Djellel Difallah, Elena Filatova and Panos Ipeirotis have conducted a 28-month survey which revealed that 'the number of available workers on Mechanical Turk is at least 100K, with approximately 2K workers being active at any given moment' (Difallah *et al.* 2018, 2). They have also demonstrated that 'the MTurk workers' half-life is 12-18 months, indicating that the population refreshes significantly over time' (2). Branded a 'virtual sweatshop', MTurk basically offers labour as performed by not yet quite artificial intelligence. The platform's name is borrowed from the late eighteenth-century chess-playing automaton constructed by Wolfgang von Kempelen and displayed at European courts and other venues of prominence. In the game of magic often associated with new technologies and the promises made in their name, tinted by the orientalist fantasies of the day, von Kempelen's automaton featured a turban-sporting sculpture ('The Turk') positioned above all sorts of contraptions that hinted at the complex mechanisms inside. Yet what the inside really hid was a human chess master, whose intelligence was needed to power the illusion of a chess-playing machine.

Given that the tasks required by Amazon's low-price anonymous labourers are infinite, it is understandable why artists may flock to the platform. Driven by opportunism, curiosity or even a desire to unveil the hidden conditions of global labour in the digital age, they have asked MTurks to 'draw a sheep facing to the left' that later made up a massive digital tapestry, paint small sections of a $100 bill without realising it was to become part of a larger picture, literally and metaphorically (both projects by Aaron Koblin), photograph themselves holding a sign which revealed why they did this work (Andy Baio) or sticking the middle finger at their webcam (Guido Segni, fig. 11), realise webcam performances (Eva and Franco Mattes) and even write poetry (Nick Thurston). There is a long history of artists exploring the multiple dimensions of creativity while challenging their own singular role in the process by 'crowdsourcing' their works – from André Breton's *Exquisite Corpse*, which involved collectively assembling words and images, through to mail art, smart mobs and Harrell Fletcher and Miranda July's LearningToLoveYouMore.com, where participants were asked to perform simple tasks (e.g. 'Take a picture of strangers holding hands') and upload the results to a website (see Grover 2006, Holmes 2011). What is new about using MTurk is that crowdsourced art is really an outcome of extremely cheap labour undertaken by those who rely on Amazon's platform for income, rather than of playful participation in a shared activity. Yet artists sometimes alleviate their conscience by believing that they offer a diversion to workers exposed to the chain of otherwise mindless HITs by allowing them to do something 'creative'.

Koblin's work has garnered particular criticism. Laboral, a Spanish Centre for Art and Industrial Creation, have argued that 'Exploitation of creative labour, albeit in a humorous way, is built into this system of participatory art making', while at the same time acknowledging that *The Sheep Market* 'questions the commodification of networked "human intelligence" and cultural production' (Laboral non-dated). M/C Elish has pointed out that in projects of this kind '[t]he implications and the stakes of Mechanical Turk as an economic system are left untouched' (Elish 2010). These implications have been addressed by many scholars of labour in the global networked economy, but it is possible to shift registers somewhat, I want to suggest, without abandoning the critical commitment. Clare Bishop's concept of 'delegated performance' offers a more nuanced reading of such practices. Bishop is not writing specifically about MTurk, but she does discuss various forms of artistic activity such as live installations and docudrama, where people hired by artists are expected 'to perform their own socioeconomic category, be this on the basis of gender, class, ethnicity, age, disability, or (more rarely) profession' (2012, 91). Rather than condemn such practices *tout court* in an act of complete political dismissal or moralistic outrage, she proposes to see delegated performance 'as an *artistic* practice engaging with the ethics and aesthetics of contemporary labor, and not simply as a micro-model of reification' (91). (Bishop does draw a line between the more multi-layered and troubling works such as those by Tino Sehgal, Artur Żmijewski and Elmgreen & Dragset, and the unwittingly self-parodic 'art-fair-art' such as the recent gallery events by Marina Abramović.)

And it is precisely in ethical terms, where ethics stands for an openness and responsibility towards the other which is not yet filled in with any positive content,[20] that we can read the work of many contemporary artists working explicitly with crowdsourced material via acts of delegated labour, I want to argue. Nick Thurston's book *Of the Subcontract* contains poems written by MTurkers as part of their HIT and is prefaced by a foreword which Marxist critic McKenzie Wark had commissioned, via Freelancer.com, from a ghost-writer in Pakistan for $75. The poems veer between naïve and self-knowing, crafty and well-crafted, but, in being framed by the MTurk pricing and the time dedicated to the fulfilment of the task, they all serve as a basic lesson in classic materialism: there is no 'pure' aesthetic experience outside the wider social conditions of labour, even if the artist or the recipient want to use the work to create an illusion of its existence. While many of the poems deal with supposedly universal topics such as pain, love and beauty, several are knowingly self-reflexive about the task – and the life – at hand:

> 0.04 *[written in response to the offered payment of 0.02 cents]*
> *Would you do work for this measly amount?*
> *Would you take it seriously, would it even count.*
> *('Am I Blind, or Maybe Dumb?', in Thurston 2013, 24)*

> *00.17 [payment of 0.17 cents]*
> *To write a poem for you*
> *That would surely not do*
> *For you to take it and make it your own.*
> *('A Poem You Did Not Write', in Thurston 2013, 38)*

Thurston's book thus foregrounds the MTurkers' conditions of labour, which turn them into an '"elastic staffing pool" to whom the employer has no obligation beyond the agreed payment' (Thurston in Voyce 2014, 105). Clone-like in their anonymity, MTurkers are 'differentiated only by their listed efficiency relative to the efficiency of the latest Master Workers, just as all computers are the computer, differentiated only by their inbuilt processing capacity relative to the capacity of the latest market-leading computers' (Thurston in Voyce, 108). The artificial artificial intelligence of the MTurk labour force is thus both a representation of the labour ideal in the times of global capital flows and a premonition of things to come, for the majority of workers, in the majority of jobs and careers. Yet the worry that AI-driven robots will take over, that they are going to replace us, is often dismissed by technocapitalists with the breezy reassurance that new jobs will be created, poverty diminished, and that, as a result of widespread automation, 'we' will simply have more free time'. The rebranding of unemployment and precarity as freedom sounds particularly ominous in the positive reports about the supposed desirability of the gig economy, with its 'flexibility' and 'freedom'. In the aptly titled article, 'The Internet Is Enabling a New Kind of Poorly Paid Hell', published in *The Atlantic* in January 2018, Alana Semuels explains:

> A research paper published in December that analyzed 3.8 million tasks on Mechanical Turk, performed by 2,676 workers, found that those workers earned a median hourly wage of about $2 an hour. Only 4 percent of workers earned more than $7.25 an hour. Kotaro Hara, the lead author of the study and a professor at Singapore Management University, told me that workers earn so little because it's hard to secure enough tasks to be working every minute they're in front of the computer. He says workers spend a lot of time looking for tasks, waiting for the interface to load, and trying to complete poorly explained tasks before deciding to return them. ... How is it legal to compensate workers so poorly? The federal minimum wage in America, after all, is $7.25 an hour. But ... crowdsourced workers do not have to receive the minimum wage because they are considered independent contractors, not employees. (Semuels 2018)

This problem of underemployment and underpayment affects not only workers on labour-sourcing platforms such as MTurk, CrowdFlower, Clickworker, Toluna or

Fiverr, but also other actors in the 'disruptive' gig economy, bankrolled by Silicon Valley capital, such as Uber and Deliveroo drivers, zero-hours contract shop assistants and, last but not least, casualised academic staff.

Darren Wershler's afterword to Thurston's *Of The Subcontract* makes an important suggestion with regard to the force of such projects. More than as a critique of a particular form of creativity (in this case, poetry, with all its forms and conventions) or even of the economics of MTurk, he suggests Thurston's project can be read as an institutional critique of the conditions of the production of art, with fame and glory attached to the singular auteur, but with the labour and infrastructure provided by 'legion'. (This applies to fine art made by the likes of Damien Hirst, to which of course there are historical antecedents predating the era of industrial capitalism – if not that of the celebration of the individual/ist human subject – as much as it does to fashion or entertainment media.) Wershler recognises Thurston's gesture as 'fully ironised' (Wershler 2013, 138), revealing as it does 'that the once-lauded cultural value of the work of poets is now so close to nothing as to be indistinguishable from it, and that the work of precarious labourers in a networked digital milieu, which is remunerated far below minimum wage, without benefits or the collective bargaining power of unionisation, is nevertheless dignified' (138). Wershler proposes to read *Of the Subcontract* not as a solution but rather as a symptom of an age in which all sorts of activities are reconfigured as Human Intelligence Tasks. This reconfiguration goes hand in hand with the full automation of typically human creative tasks such as reporting, journalism and data analysis, with a growing list of jobs and careers threatened by being lost to AI. 'Poets and professors can point to this change', says Wershler, 'but, so far, have not been able to move beyond it. As we are beginning to realise, our tasks, too, can be outsourced' (139). This state of events, deemed 'the uberfication of the university' by Gary Hall in his eponymous book (2016b), hints at a near-future in which we all become 'entrepreneurs of the self', with every aspect of our lives – from inhabiting a room or sleeping on someone's sofa, making friends and dating through to walking – monetised both as a 'shareable' good and a data point. Yet any wealth generated as part of this so-called sharing economy is 'concentrated in the hands of relatively few', who 'also centrally control the platform, software, algorithm, data, and associated ecosystem, deciding on pricing and wage levels, work allocation, standards, conditions, and preferred user and laborer profiles' (Hall 2016b).

Significantly, Hall offers more than just a critique of the precarious labour conditions in the digital economy – or of the extension of these conditions to professions and careers that were previously seen as safe from the disruptive logic of its algorithms: Wershler's 'poets and professors'. He also issues a call to arms aimed at those *in* the academic world, highlighting that the university – and, we may also add, its more creative variant, the art school – 'provides one of the few spaces in postindustrial society where the forces of contemporary neoliberalism's anti-public sector regime are still being overtly opposed, to a certain extent at least' (2016b). The most important question we are posed with here is not therefore whether robots and algorithms *can* replace us as artists, poets and professors. Although, to answer that underlying question, 'they' surely can – by being able to produce singular artefacts that will 'take us in', evoke the sensation of beauty, become popular or even sell well, and by producing online books, classes and whole courses made up of the existing and rehashed content that 'will do', for a while at least. The question rather is how to create conditions in which creativity with its accompanying institutions, especially those not driven by the logic of innovation, profit and capital – institutions such as public universities and art schools, state-owned galleries, museums and cultural centres – still count *for us embodied humans with material and other needs.*

The belief in the wisdom of the crowd associated with the optimism of the early Internet era, and driven by the spirit of communitarianism and collaboration, has lost its shine in the age of global digital surveillance, fake news, Twitter bubbles and the possible election manipulation via social media. The crowd has now been revealed to be not so much wise as mouldable and subject to all sorts of exploitation. We have also learnt not only that 'they' are really watching us but also that we are all doing it to one another: we are all MTurks in Jeff Bezos' or Mark Zuckerberg's digital factories. Crowdsourcing therefore becomes a form of crowd-mobbing. And thus, even if I argue that we have always been artificially intelligent, the specific historical and cultural labour practices of humans at a given point in time do matter. *View from the Window* thus can be seen as an indictment of inhumane labour practices, of the supposed ease with which an erasure of the human is being enacted. In its photographic legacy and epistemological ambition to see otherwise, it casts light on the lingering shadows of the globalised digital labour market. Presented as diptychs in an automated photobook, the project foregrounds the mediation processes shaping the production of knowledge, while also revealing the human signal points involved in the process. We see in them different labour distribution from what look like the suburbs in the US, possibly in India, maybe somewhere in Latin America. Through the uneasy parallelism of the image pairs, the work asks whose interests are bring represented – and who can afford to be creative, where, when and for how long.

The defence of art practices and institutions for the human offered in this chapter has little to do with any residual humanism, a desire to preserve 'our human uniqueness', 'our sense of beauty' or any other humanist niceties of this kind. Instead, it has to do with asking poets and professors to keep fighting against the uberfication of the university and the art school, of knowledge production and art production. With *View from the Window*, and the wider project of undigital photography, I thus want to show that, even though we are all entangled in algorithms, it matters how we use them, what visions and vistas they will be made to produce, who will get to see them, who (or what) will takes the picture, of what, in what circumstances, to what purpose and for what price. Building on the legacy of the term in computer science, undigital photography thus becomes for me a way of reframing the picture after it's been taken, of looking askew and anew, of refocusing and re-zooming on what matters, and of rethinking what matters to begin with. It is also a way of seeing photography and image making as a practices that are inherently unfinished. And thus, even though *View from the Window* does point to the constraints of globalised outsourced labour, it also returns agency *and pleasure* to the workers as producers of worlds *and* worldviews. Through this, it echoes Bishop's conviction that 'people relentlessly exceed the categories under which they have been recruited' (2012, 111).[21] Moving beyond the uniqueness of the single image on a gallery wall or the predictability of the Instagram flow, the project of undigital photography becomes an ethico-political opening towards the unknown, coupled with a demand for this knowledge not to be computed too quickly.

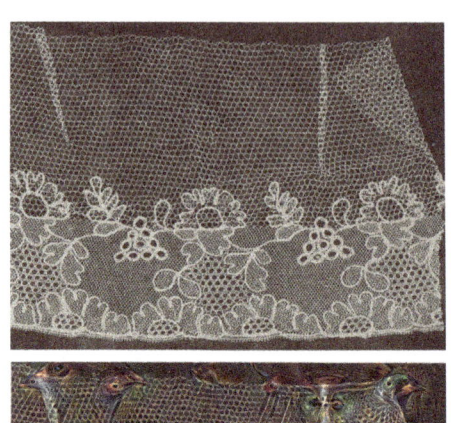
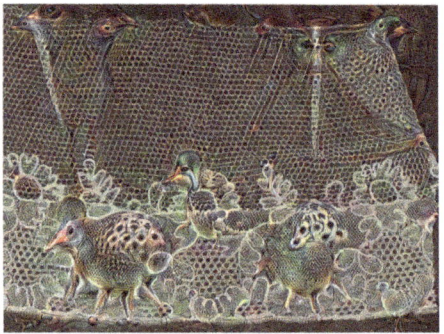
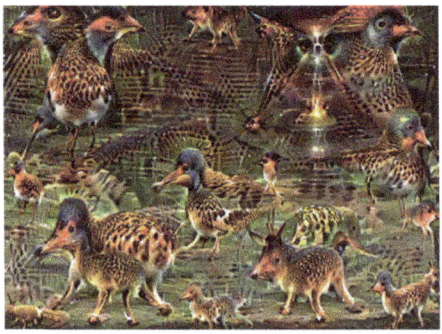

Fig. 12. William Henry Fox Talbot's Lace from *The Pencil of Nature*, 1845 – an image that arguably hints at photography's quintessentially algorithmic, pattern-based legacy (Batchen 2001, 169; Zylinska 2017, 182) – remediated by Joanna Zylinska via Google's DeepDream, 2018.

CHAPTER II

From Net Art and Post-Internet Art to Artificially Intelligent Art – and Beyond

Having looked at some specific examples of AI art, including my own attempt to engage with the issue on a practical level, in this chapter I begin to emerge on the other side of the book's funnel-like structure by opening up once again towards some bigger issues concerning human and nonhuman creativity. In chapter 5 I considered robotic art, and its experiments in machinic creativity, as a predecessor of AI-driven art. Here I want to situate AI art within the lineage of some earlier forms of media art that have engaged with computer networks, such as net art and post-Internet art.

Having burst onto the media scene in the early to mid-1990s, net art consisted of works made on and for the Internet by individuals and collectives who had an advanced understanding of the new medium – and who were keen to explore this medium in an irreverent and critical way. Part artists, part activists, net artists had a sharp understanding of the potential of the new medium and of its yet undefined boundaries and modes of operation. The net art moment was generative and, inevitably perhaps, short-lasting. When the term 'post-Internet'[22] art started appearing in gallery writeups and art blogs in the early 2010s, it referred to work produced by artists who had come of age surrounded by digital technology – and whose sense of novelty and curiosity about the digital medium was therefore less pronounced than that of the previous generation of net artists.[23] The gradual immersion of not just artists but also the wider population in the digital ecosystem of the Internet, coupled with the simplification and automation of digital interfaces, brought with it more than just greater ease with technological apparatuses and infrastructures, the sense of being 'always on' and having much of culture available 'on tap'. It also arguably led to the vanishing of the Brechtian *Verfremdungseffekt*[24] with regard to digital technology, precisely because the digital milieu had turned out not to be so alien any more, at least on the surface. Instead, the so-called 'digital natives' began to swim through the waters of digital technology like the aquatic creatures from an anecdote recounted by David Foster Wallace in a 2005 college commencement speech. On being greeted by an older fish swimming past them, 'Morning, boys, how's the water?', the two young fish could only respond with: 'What the hell is water?' (Wallace 2008). With this anecdote, Wallace wanted to convey to the students the importance of becoming more aware of their surroundings: the 'default setting' they use to make their way through the world, the ideologies that shape this world, the myths and meanings transmitted by those ideologies.

Much of the discussion around 'post-Internet' art, encapsulated by artist Artie Vierkant's 2010 essay, 'The Image Object Post-Internet', focused precisely on this tension between familiarity and ignorance, with artists stepping in to deliver a critical commentary on the (by then overly familiar yet still strange) digital milieu. That commentary took the form of blogposts, pamphlets and panels but it also extended to the production of artworks which took their digital provenance for granted while exploring their uncertain and hybrid ontology: from Oliver Laric's 3D-printed casts of classic Greek and Roman sculptures through to Jon Rafman's alien-looking busts covered with digitally remastered works of Picasso, Rothko or Kandinsky, images of which had been taken from the Internet. Post-Internet art was thus 'inherently informed by ubiquitous authorship, the development of attention as currency, the collapse of physical space in networked culture, and the infinite reproducibility and mutability of digital materials', with artists taking on 'a role more closely aligned to that of the interpreter, transcriber, narrator, curator, architect' (Vierkant 2010). It is therefore rather ironic that the hybrid materiality of post-Internet art was quickly absorbed by the logic of the traditional gallery circuit, with art dealers and gallery owners breathing a sigh of relief because they once again had physical objects to show and sell.

The demands of AI art replicate those of early net art to some extent, in the sense that a certain level of technical expertise is required to be able to get involved in the practice. At the same time, the conditions of its production are very different. The political economy of the Internet and of the wider technological infrastructures has changed, with the utopian idea of the world wide web as the commons giving way to proprietary warfare between tech companies, media moguls and political actors over the ownership of data, machines, bodies and minds. There is therefore less scope for the cultivation of the 'tinkering ethos' of net art, with its hacker affinities and collaborative spirit. Much of current AI art, driven by the engineering mindset, comes from a very different place: sometimes it literally comes from Google. The alienation effect caused by AI tends to be swept away by visual transmogrification that actually prevents understanding rather than enhancing it. Indeed, as I argued earlier on in this book, much of the current AI art – or at least the works that gain visibility at festivals, fairs and with the wider public – has been reduced to a pure spectacle, underwritten by the following message: *you don't need to understand it because you are already in it*. It could therefore be described as 'artificially intelligent art'. Even though the conditions of the emergence of AI to some extent resemble those of the early days of the Internet in terms of the need for advanced know-how if one is to delve into the emergent technological infrastructure, the anthropomorphised (and often feminised) banality of digital interfaces creates an illusion of familiarity and comfort.

Such 'artificially intelligent art', i.e. art which reduces expertise to engineering competency while foreclosing on the (artist's and user's) critical engagement at the expense of offering a stunning visual spectacle, is of course not the only way of creatively engaging with AI, even if this is the kind of art that features prominently in AI-focused shows. Lauren McCarthy's project *Lauren!* offers a different take on artificial intelligence, both as a technology and discourse. The artist installs custom-designed networked smart devices such as cameras, microphones, switches, door locks and taps in willing participants' homes. She then engages in the constant monitoring of them, while being of assistance in response to requests to switch on the light or advise whether someone needs a haircut. Through these banal acts of digitally-mediated outsourcing of everyday activities, McCarthy attempts 'to become a human version of Amazon Alexa, a smart home intelligence' (McCarthy 2017) for people in their own abodes. The artist explores human-machine interaction through the lens of playfulness, irony and pastiche, demystifying the grand promises behind some of AI, while also raising the question of the willing suspension of privacy – which only starts feeling weird when the spying is undertaken by a 'human Alexa'. She explains that people 'are usually expecting more technical tricks at first, a real sci-fi experience. But much like smart homes of today, I mostly do what they could do themselves – things like flipping switches, playing music, and looking up answers. ... By allowing these devices in, we outsource the formation of our identity to a virtual assistant whose values are programmed by a small, homogenous group of developers' (McCarthy 2018). While foregrounding the narrowness of algorithms and the vested interests of tech companies in selling us all those digital butlers, McCarthy raises broader questions about how 'individuation' happens in the age of AI: i.e. how we become human in relation with technical objects. The technical origin of the human has been posited by philosophers such as Gilbert Simondon and Bernard Stiegler, with individuation being understood by the latter as an ongoing process of an individual emerging from a techno-social ensemble, rather than creating this ensemble *ex nihilo*. 'Simondon says that if you want to understand the individual, you need to inscribe the individual in a process of which he is only a phase' (Stiegler and Rogoff 2010). For Stiegler, multiple individuals are permanently in the process of being constituted (and re-constituted), relating to and being dependent on, one another – with not all of those 'others' always being human (see Stiegler 1998 and Simondon 2016). What McCarthy's project therefore allows us to interrogate in this ongoing process of human becoming (with) AI is what kind of technology we enter into a relationship with, in whose interest, and to what effect and purpose. She also implores us to ask: What kind of 'phases' are constituted through AI encounters? What kind of AI emerges *from* those encounters?

Through engaging in a series of banal everyday tasks McCarthy reveals the uncomfortable fact that the 'The scale of resources required is many magnitudes greater than the energy and labor it would take a human to operate a household appliance or flick a switch' (Crawford and Joler 2018). Each such 'small moment of convenience', to use Kate Crawford and Vladan Joler's term, 'requires a vast planetary network, fueled by the extraction of non-renewable materials, labor, and data' (Crawford and Joler 2018). We are all unpaid labourers in the AI industry, McCarthy seems to suggest, being seduced by promises of convenience, assistance or simply 'fun' to engage on a daily basis in servicing the data economy, finetuning its algorithms and expanding its reach. As Crawford and Joler point out, 'In the dynamic of dataset collection through platforms like Facebook, users are feeding and training the neural networks with behavioral data, voice, tagged pictures and videos or medical data' (2018). We could therefore suggest that McCarthy denaturalises 'the digital water' of AI technology for us by shifting some of the labour of the technological ensemble to the human – who becomes a witness, a spy, a police(wo)man and a moral conscience as part of her act. With this, she can be said to be challenging Silicon Valley's delusionism and hydrophobia, which I defined in chapter 3 as the wariness of the elemental side of media technology. By implicitly responding to the Anthropocene Imperative, McCarthy shows us an opening towards another engagement with AI – and towards another world that may just about be possible.

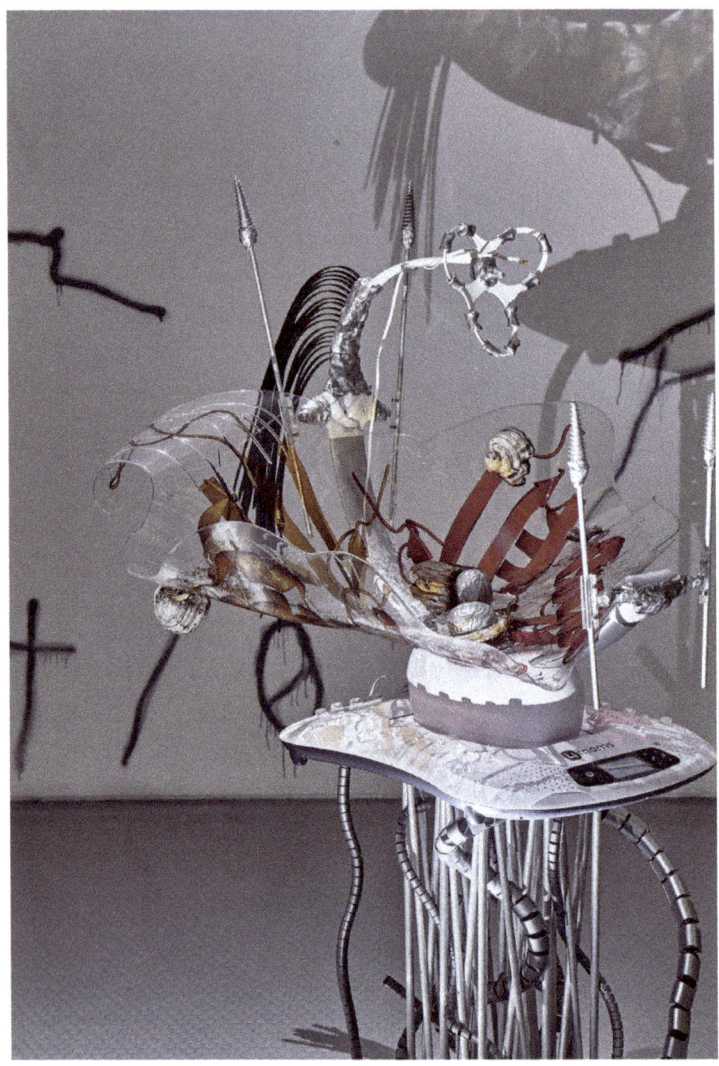

Fig. 13. Katja Novitskova, detail of installation *Pattern of Activation* (Mamaroo nursery, dawn chorus), from exhibition for Preis der Nationalgalerie at Hamburger Bahnhof, Berlin, 2019. Installation photography by def-image. Courtesy of the artist and Kraupa-Tuskany Zeidler.

CHAPTER 12

AI as Another Intelligence

While McCarthy wants to make the digital everyday uncomfortable, Katja Novitskova seemingly has the opposite goal. In the foreword to her 2010 edited art book, *Post Internet Survival Guide*, the Estonian artist writes: 'the Internet is an invisible given, like roads or trees, and is used to navigate not just information but also matter and space. The notion of a survival guide arises as an answer to a basic human need to cope with increasing complexity. In the face of death, personal attachment and confusion, one has to feel, interpret and index this ocean of signs in order to survive' (Novitskova 2010). Challenging our supposed seamless immersion in digital culture, she wants us to see the water – through which she shares with Lauren McCarthy the desire to denaturalise our environment. Novitskova took this spirit to her project, *If Only You Could See What I've Seen with Your Eyes* (fig. 13), first exhibited at 57th Venice Biennale in 2017 and then presented in different iterations at KUMU in Estonia and the Whitechapel Gallery in London in 2018. The raw material of Novitskova's practice comes from the flow of images available on the Internet: a space the artist describes as 'an exciting digital jungle' (Lavrador 2017a, 40). The project explores the incredulity of scientific knowledge and perception, engaging human and nonhuman vision to tell a playfully chilling story about a future that may have already happened. In the post-Internet spirit of the artist's earlier work, there are objects everywhere on display: from an eyeless photocopied polar bear cutout through to wires wriggling like serpents on the floor, flashing lights at us. In an attempt to provide order to this cornucopia of things that look like they've been photocopied or 3D-printed from the Internet, the exhibition space teems with labels, descriptions, snippets of information and bits of data – from the extinction diagram to ominous-sounding messages such as 'bias encoded', 'mania phase' and 'wild type mutant'. Yet, moving from room to room, we are none the wiser, for which we only have ourselves to blame as we allow ourselves to be distracted by a nature video or a revolving piece of shimmering Perspex.

Novitskova's project feels like a spoof version of the 'artificially intelligent' work which mesmerises and seduces the viewer. Yet there is no visual seduction here: instead, the visitor to her strange archive of images and objects is faced with a set of puzzles. What are these electronic cradles doing here? And what's happened to the human babies they were meant to be cradling? What do the alien-like creatures hovering above them stand for? Like a funnier version of Kazuo Ishiguro's *Never Let Me Go*, Novitskova's post-Internet dystopia has been described by Toke Lykkeberg as 'art for another intelligence' (Lykkeberg 2017, 28). The artefacts included in the exhibition may cause a sense of information overload in a human visitor, but algorithms will be able to detect immediately what a given piece of data indicates. As Lykkeberg points out, 'what the viewer therefore encounters is nothing but a meeting with their own ignorance; an ignorance that might however leave us with the glimmer of a feeling that another intelligence might yet get it' (29). Novitskova's work offers a premonition of the world to come, a world in which not only the majority of images are not being taken with a human viewer in mind – an issue that preoccupies Trevor Paglen too – but also one in which machines constantly perceive, communicate with and exist for other machines. Lykkeberg describes Novitskova's project as looking as if it had been 'made by and for who's next' (40). We could therefore perhaps suggest that, drawing on nonhuman databases and modes of perception, Novitskova creates work for an artificial intelligence which is not here yet, inviting a speculation on the future of different species. This is AI read as Another Intelligence. In this context, her extinction diagrams copied from the Internet gain a new dimension – and a new audience.

In *The Death of the PostHuman: Essays on Extinction* Claire Colebrook raises a number of thought-provoking issues:

> What happens if one thinks of the vision of no one, of the human world without humans that is still there to be seen? What remains might

> still take the form of 'a' vision or referring eye – the scene of a human world as if viewed without any body. The positing of an anthropocene era (or the idea that the human species will have marked the planet to such a degree that we will be discernible as a geological strata) deploys the idea of human imaging – the way we have already read an inhuman past in the earth's layers – but does this by imagining a world in which humans will be extinct. The anthropocene thought experiment also alters the modality of geological reading, not just to refer to the past as it is for us, but also to our present as it will be without us. We imagine a viewing or reading in the absence of viewers or readers, and we do this through images in the present that extinguish the dominance of the present. (Colebrook 2014, 28)

Colebrook identifies a paradox at the heart of much of 'Anthropocene art' being produced today in response to climate change and the threat of extinction of various species – including our own. Banal representationalist works aside, even the more experimental artistic practices inevitably end up reaffirming the cognitive-sensory apparatus of the human as reader, perceiver and 'experiencer'. Yet many of the more interesting works, amongst which I locate Novitskova's project, do attempt to enact a defamiliarisation of not just 'the environment' (by showing it as damaged, disappearing or already gone) but also of us humans as recipients of sensations from the environment conceived in a broader sense – and of which we are part. It is indeed in that latter practice of imagining a world for a different recipient that a radical critical gesture can be identified.

We could therefore perhaps argue that some of the most interesting work that engages with artificial intelligence today occupies that parergonal space we identified earlier in Paglen's image-based practice. Yet its force lies somewhere else than in an attempt to reveal the mechanisms of power behind the system. 'In many cases, transparency wouldn't help much' anyway, as Crawford and Joler point out, because 'without forms of real choice, and corporate accountability, mere transparency won't shift the weight of the current power asymmetries' (Crawford and Joler 2018). Whether shifting such weight is an achievable or even desirable task for art is a topic for a different project, although my argument – and that of the MEDIA : ART : WRITE : NOW book series in which it is placed, with the sense of urgency encapsulated by its title – does share post-Internet art's embracing of the conviction that 'Art is a social object' (Vierkant 2010). The point I am making here rather conveys a suspicion on my part towards the more bombastic claims with regard to art's efficacy in solving social ills, 'empowering' communities or 'causing' change by revealing injustice. This is not to say that art should not ever attempt to do the latter, only that artists themselves could perhaps curb somewhat their own exuberant beliefs and pronouncements. The efficacy of art that engages with AI lies perhaps first and foremost in its ability to redraft the conceptual and discursive boundaries of human perception, human value and human cultural practice, while drawing us as its human recipients into the recognition of our becoming (with) machines. Such art can also make our human intelligence look inherently artificial – not only because it relies on technological prostheses such as canes, phones and implants to accomplish things but also because it is a product of relations, or, as Colebrook puts it, because 'we are *only* organizing relations. There is not a self who perceives; there are perceptions, from which something like a self is constituted' (Colebrook 2014, 17-18). With this, she challenges the pre-modern view of the human (which we have never fully left behind) that elevates the human above the other species by seeing us as 'more than' just animalistic appetites, and that understands our human mode of being as being 'responsible for out organizing relation to the world' (17). For Colebrook, echoing the work of philosophy developed by Henri Bergson and Gilles Deleuze but also picked up by some sections of cognitive science, perceptions and images precede the emergence of the self – which is only constituted *through* perceiving and imagining.

Intelligent work on artificial intelligence could therefore perhaps attempt to sever that link between the work of art and human vision, going beyond the mere *aesthesis* of human experience to open up the problem of the universe itself as sentient. 'It is not the case that we begin life as observing, representing beings who then become through receptivity. Rather, in the beginning is a dynamic and world-oriented receptivity from which organised cognition, and the sense of the self as subject or man emerges. It is from a primary openness to the world, a primarily sensed world, that there emerges the sense of one who sees' (Colebrook 2014, 20). Yet how this intelligence will be enacted, what relations it will enter into and what modulations they will gain at a given moment in time turns into an aesthetic and ethical problem for us transient but not-yet-extinct humans, here and now.

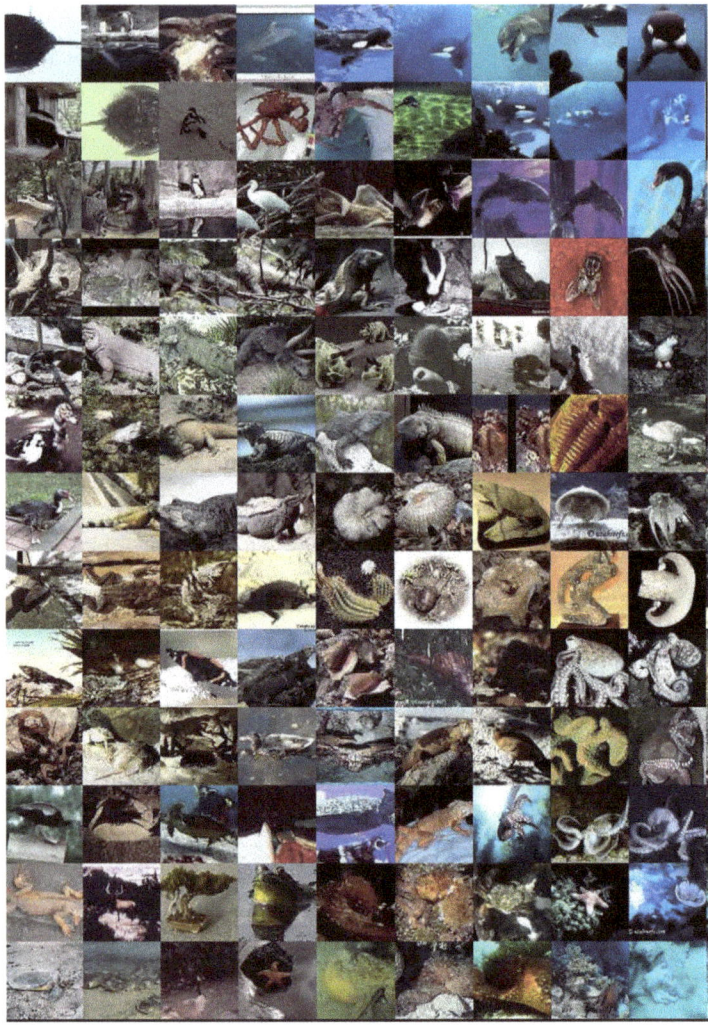

Fig. 14. Partial screenshot from browser of the t-SNE Viewer applied to a grid of animal images, available in the 'Demos' section of the ml4a (Machine Learning for Artists) open-source/community tutorial website. T-SNE stands for a 't-Distributed Stochastic Neighbor Embedding' and is an algorithmic technique, developed by Laurens van der Maaten and Geoffrey Hinton, which is particularly useful for the visualisation of high-dimensional data sets.

Future Art, Art's Future: A Conclusion

Through its design philosophy and the ideas fuelling its application, AI invites speculation about the future: not just the future of art but also our human future. In *AI Art* I have taken up this invitation by attempting to explore a wider horizon of futurity opened up by both technologies and discourses of AI. Yet my book is very much anchored in the present moment. It looks specifically at art being made with, around or in response to the current developments in robotics, machine vision and deep learning, at a time when AI research has emerged rejuvenated from the 'winter' period of the late 1980s-1990s and is now once again a growing field. As already stated, the field's growth has been accompanied by voluminous promises – and multiple threats. As much as in the artefacts produced for display across different platforms, media and institutions, I have been interested in the financial, rhetorical and affective investments in AI 2.0. My ambition in this book has therefore been to look at AI-driven art *here and now*, while situating it in the context of wider socio-political and ecological issues. It has also been to address, implicitly, the following questions: If AI is a game changer, what is actually the game? And who runs the game parlour? An inquiry into what *future* AI art will look like therefore necessarily has to consider a much bigger yet also impossible to answer question (unless attempted on the level of speculative fiction) of what *everything else* will look like. And, following that, of who, or what, will be doing the looking.

On a more modest scale an attempt to address the future of art and other creative forms driven by AI has been made by Lev Manovich is his short 2018 book *AI Aesthetics*. Manovich points out that already today many of us rely on AI 'to automate our aesthetic choices (via recommendation engines)' or even engage in aesthetic production (e.g. by relying on algorithms embedded in our mobile phones' software to produce professional-looking photos with great ease). He also claims that in the future AI 'will play a larger part in professional cultural production' (Manovich 2018). Much of what he proposes is based on the previously discussed idea of computers being better at processing large data sets and seeing connections that may not be obvious for the human, although he is aware that those connections may not actually be recognisable, or simply interesting, *for* the human. There is, however, a foundational blind spot entailed in Manovich's proposition that AI may 'suggest new ways of seeing culture' (Manovich 2018), which is premised on AI running its operations silently in the background of the ensemble, with the constitutive parts of that ensemble – 'humans', 'perception', 'valorisation', 'culture' – remaining intact. Unless we are satisfied with the rather superficial observations about the colour palette of different films or the typology of smiles in selfies posted on Instagram, and with the constant deferral of critical interpretation of not just the data but the very technology and idea of producing and displaying the data (see Hall 2016a, 43-55), we have to conclude that Manovich's project of AI enhancing variability is rather limited in what it is able to reveal. The question about an increase in 'aesthetic variability' as a result of 'AI integration in cultural production and reception' (Manovich 2018) thus actually misses the point because it is premised on a static notion of both culture and the human subject. In other words, Manovich's project of AI aesthetics (which is an extension of his Cultural Analytics)[25] remains oblivious of the fact that data does not just map things out as they objectively are prior to being mapped, but in fact constitutes reality. So, instead of envisaging The Human 2.0 as a producer and recipient of AI art in terms of a slightly expanded and diversified version of the current human, what would it mean to think seriously about the future of AI – for art, for human sensation and experience, and for the world as we know it, in all its nonhuman entanglements?

Alongside the 'more of the same but bigger' trend, alternative scenarios for AI futures have swung from dystopian stories about an AI breakout and the subsequent human enslavement and extinction, to utopian visions in which all labour and drudgery will be eliminated and all humans will be free to pursue their passions and exercise their creativity. But it is not so much AI futures that should worry us but rather the AI present: a time when not only do we have access to more variegated data but also when we ourselves have all become data subjects, with our 'behavioural surplus' constantly feeding into the machinery of what Shoshana Zuboff calls 'surveillance capitalism' (see Zuboff 2019). The question is therefore whether our future has already been spent or whether it can still be redeemed. In his book *Futurability: The Age of Impotence and the Horizon of Possibility*, with which I opened my line of enquiry in this volume, Franco 'Bifo' Berardi has postulated 'the multiplicity of immanent possible futures' (Berardi 2017). The present moment, with its ecological and economic destructions, and the material and discursive havoc wreaked upon our planet, seems to suggest humanity is on a downward trajectory, that it has already ordered in its own expiration. Yet, contrary to the predictions of the various fetishists of the apocalypse, I want to follow Bifo in arguing that our shared future has not yet been totally spent, irrevocably conquered or deterministically designed. And so, amidst the ruin of our current political thought, a possibility of another, more utopian, future can perhaps be sought and fought for.

This possibility of envisaging a different future and painting a different picture of the world may require us to extend an invitation to nonhuman others to join the project and help redraft its aesthetic boundaries. Pierre

Huyghe's *UUmwelt* could be seen as an attempt to achieve precisely this. The work, displayed at the Serpentine Galleries in London in 2018-2019, presented visitors with multiple LED screens showing flickering blurry images of different classes of beings and objects. The exhibition was set up as an environment (or *Umwelt*, following the biosemiotician Jakob von Uexküll's term, to which Huyghe added another U in a playful attempt at defamiliarisation, breech or even negation) made up of human, animal and technological agents. Specifically, it was constituted by deep neural networks, image databases serving as learning material for those networks, scans of human brains, flies buzzing around the gallery while getting trapped in the visitors' hair and hats, and the visitors themselves – as well as layers of history and art history, visualised as dust scraped off the gallery's walls. This additional U of the title was meant to signal the internal discord of any environment as a dynamic in which many entities are co-present but do not perceive the world in the same way or actually even *share* that world in any meaningful sense of the word.[26] The images presented on the screens were supposedly the outcome of a translation process undertaken by the neural networks, which attempted to interpret the data from human fMRI brain scans and produce a sequence of pictures on that basis. *UUmwelt* was thus an attempt for a computer to see the way humans see, and thus to enact an encounter between two kinds of intelligence, with all the poetic and technical ambivalences this exercise in inevitable mistranslation entailed.

The Serpentine's environment contained multiple ecologies of different rhythms and scales interacting with one another, often inadvertently and indifferently, largely outside or even beyond human intentionality and control. The neural networks involved in the creation of novel images on the basis of familiar ones opened up the possibility of seeing otherwise – for both the machine *and* the human. Nonhuman vision became a much-needed corrective to the humanist viewpoint, with its perspectival mastery and possessive gaze. Indeed, *UUmwelt* revealed the incompatibility of visions of different species, while foregrounding the uncertainty and tenuousness of environmental coexistence. Experimentation with seeing otherwise, and with exploring seemingly incompatible environments – not just between humans and machines but also across the human-nonhuman spectrum which is always already biotechnological (geological faultlines, species boundaries, immigration lines, legality, walls, borders) – became a metaphor for our current socio-political moment, in all its planetary specificity and fragility. As Huyghe himself put it: 'You set conditions, but you cannot define the outcome…' (Huyghe 2018).

The immanence of multiple possible futures does not thus come with any guarantees. Indeed, some future scenarios have been embedded, developed and funded better, bringing in an era of what Hito Steyerl has called an artificial stupidity, 'a mediocre and greedy version of the sublime machine intelligence intended to elevate and improve human life' (Steyerl 2018). Yet even if technology, including AI, cannot be seen as a fix, nor should it be reduced to the role of a demon. Critical and speculative AI work shows the limits of our vision, of our viewpoints and standpoints. Indeed, it shows them precisely as viewpoints rather than as absolute truths. Image production unfolding between these two kinds of intelligence reveals that our human intelligence is always already plural, with us being entangled with microbes, fungi, DNA fossils, cosmic dust as well as layerings of culture, upbringing, personal and sociocultural umwelt. AI projects of this kind can remind us that 'the way we interpret the world is specific only to us' (Huyghe 2018). The multiplicity and fragmentariness of the *UUmwelt* images, shown in rapid succession, always in a different arrangement, reveal that there may be no unified 'us' either, for better or for worse.

'We' thus find ourselves at a curious moment in time, a time when AI research has woken up from its many winters and is being touted as both the ultimate threat and the ultimate promise. In the final paragraphs of this book I would like to loop back to this book's opening questions – questions about the ontological and technological specificity of AI art, about its purpose and about the present and future audiences for such art. They all lead to the fundamental question concerning the very possibility of art's existence *after* AI – and, indeed, of the existence of anything else. Having posed so many big questions throughout the course of this slim volume, it may seem unfair to leave them here without some more definitive answers. However, the main idea behind my book has been to show how the very act of questioning can equip us with tools for cutting through the smoke and mirrors surrounding the AI hype, with its machinic visions and warped dreams. And thus the question of what art 'after AI' and, more broadly, posthuman art, could look like perhaps requires a reassessment of the standpoint from which this question can actually be asked, coupled with the rescaling of our human worldview, here and now. It also requires a reflection on the cultural, social and economic dimension of our human practices, including that of 'art', with all its historical assessments, financial valuations, collective sensations, singular pleasures and, last but not least, market and stylistic inflations.

A return to the human scale in the closing pages of this book must not be confused with a desire to reinstate humanism, or posit human modes of assessment, analysis and appreciation as dominant or superior. Indeed, as we know from recent work in cognitive psychology, evolutionary biology and neuroscience, intelligence and perception can be found across the existent evolutionary spectrum, at levels much more complex and more developed than we have realised for centuries, even if they do not always present themselves to us humans as such. So it is not a matter of just inviting 'others' to our human cognitive and sensory circle, or expanding the definition of art so that 'they' can be included too. My closing proposal is actually much more modest: we need to open up the human sensorium to other forms of intelligence and perception, to recognise our entanglement with creatures and machines, to look around, askew. This opening needs to involve our recognition of the human capacity for telling stories, having visions and dreaming dreams. Yet it also has to take up the ethical task of acknowledging our ability to reflect on those stories, visions and dreams critically, while widely awake. Because, as Donna Haraway has poignantly highlighted, 'It matters what thoughts think thoughts. It matters what knowledges know knowledges. ... It matters what stories tell stories' (2016, 35). In other words, it matters what we see, show and tell, about whom, with what, and why. Art is one human practice where the mattering of matter, and of matters that (should) matter, can be explored in an affective, effective and non-moralistic way.

(Art) Gallery of Links

This is a list of links to the online versions of the art projects discussed in the book, and to the selected artists' websites, presented in the order in which they are discussed in the book.[27]

Robot Art competition:
https://robotart.org/

Reimagine AI / Human Impact Lab, *The Climate Clock*:
https://climateclock.net/

VoidLab, *Shapeshifting AI*:
https://vimeo.com/231779659/

Artistes et Robots at Grand Palais exhibition page (archived):
https://www.grandpalais.fr/en/event/artists-robots/

Harold Cohen, *AARON*:
http://aaronshome.com/

Leonel Moura, *Robot Art*:
http://www.leonelmoura.com/bebot_works/

The Next Rembrandt:
https://www.nextrembrandt.com/

Gene Kogan, artist's website:
http://genekogan.com/

Mike Tyka, artist's website:
http://www.miketyka.com/

Mario Klingemann, artist's website:
http://quasimondo.com/

Memo Akten, *Learning to See*:
http://www.memo.tv/portfolio/learning-to-see/

Trevor Paglen, *It Began as a Military Experiment*:
https://www.moma.org/collection/works/275173/

Trevor Paglen's *Sight Machine* with Kronos Quartet and Obscura Digital:
https://vimeo.com/205149078/

Aaron Koblin, *The Sheep Market*:
http://www.aaronkoblin.com/project/the-sheep-market/

Aaron Koblin, *10,000 Cents*:
http://www.aaronkoblin.com/project/10000-cents/

Lauren McCarthy, *Lauren!*
http://lauren-mccarthy.com/LAUREN/

Katja Novitskova, *If Only You Could See What I've Seen with Your Eyes*
https://ifonlyyoucouldseewhativeseenwithyoureyes.com/

Pierre Huyghe, UUmwelt:
https://www.serpentinegalleries.org/exhibitions-events/pierre-huyghe-uumwelt/

Notes

1 Southern's claim is not quite accurate. The 2016 software AIVA, which stands for 'Artificial Intelligence Virtual Artist', is an electronic composer recognised by the French music royalties company SACEM. In November 2016 AIVA released its classical music-inspired album *Genesis*.

2 Competition announcement, https://consumer.huawei.com/uk/campaign/sparkarenaissance/, accessed March 4, 2019.

3 In his essay 'What Is an Author?', originally written in 1969, an essay which has had a significant resonance in many areas of arts and humanities, Foucault suggests that

> the 'author-function' is tied to the legal and institutional systems that circumscribe, determine, and articulate the realm of discourses; it does not operate in a uniform manner in all discourses, at all times, and in any given culture; it is not defined by the spontaneous attribution of a text to its creator, but through a series of precise and complex procedures; it does not refer, purely and simply, to an actual individual insofar as it simultaneously gives rise to a variety of egos and to a series of subjective positions that individuals of any class may come to occupy. (1992, 309)

4 Barrat goes so far as to claim that defining intelligence as something computable was shared by 'every expert' he spoke to (2013, 163).

5 The original idea for this chapter was developed in a short piece titled 'Beyond Heaven and Hell: How to tell better stories about AI', which I wrote for the online journal *Immerse* and which was published on March 29, 2018.

6   I addressed the limitations of traditional moral theory with regard to current conceptual and technological developments in *Bioethics in the Age of New Media* (2009).

7   I developed this argument in *The End of Man: A Feminist Counterapocalypse* (2018).

8   For an interesting account of elemental media, which examines the foundational yet partly invisible elements such as water, earth, fire and air that lie at the base of our habitat, while situating them in the wider context of media and communications theory due to their function as binding or, indeed, communicating, elements, see John Durham Peters, *The Marvelous Clouds: Toward a Philosophy of Elemental Media* (2015).

9   See http://www.humanimpactlab.com/the-rising-seas

10 This is part of an announcement that appeared on the Microsoft website, with the embedded quote coming from Microsoft director Ron Augustus, https://news.microsoft.com/europe/features/next-rembrandt/

11 Posting by Joseph Rabie on January 21, 2018, 14:17, to a moderated mailing list for net criticism <nettime>. Subject: They know not what they do.

12 The argument presented in this section is partly borrowed and developed from my book *Nonhuman Photography* (2017, 77).

13 This is a paraphrase, for the purposes of my argument here, of the following statement: '*the imagination of the camera is greater than that of every single photographer and that of all photographers put together*' (Flusser 2000, 30).

14 Still and d'Inverno's proposal involves the following theses: 'Adopt an N-creative approach to designing systems supporting being in the world; enhancing and supporting human creative activity in all of its forms (d'Inverno and McCormack, 2015) [and...] Use human experience as the starting point for future system design (Yee-King and d'Inverno, 2016)' (2016).

15 As Crawford and Paglen explain,
    Datasets aren't simply raw materials to feed algorithms, but are political interventions. As such, much of the discussion around 'bias' in AI systems misses the

mark: there is no 'neutral', 'natural', or 'apolitical' vantage point that training data can be built upon. There is no easy technical 'fix' by shifting demographics, deleting offensive terms, or seeking equal representation by skin tone. The whole endeavor of collecting images, categorizing them, and labeling them is itself a form of politics, filled with questions about who gets to decide what images mean and what kinds of social and political work those representations perform. (2019)

16   I am grateful to Nick Thurston for this suggestion.

17   Presentation by Fei-Fei Li at the ImageNet 10th Birthday Party event at The Photographers' Gallery in London on September 21, 2019.

18   As Crawford and Paglen explain,
ImageNet became the basis for an annual competition where labs around the world would try to outperform each other by pitting their algorithms against the training set, and seeing which one could most accurately label a subset of images. In 2012, a team from the University of Toronto used a Convolutional Neural Network to handily win the top prize, bringing new attention to this technique. That moment is widely considered a turning point in the development of contemporary AI.... The final year of the ImageNet competition was 2017, and accuracy in classifying objects in the limited subset had risen from 71.8% to 97.3%. (Crawford and Paglen, 2019)

19   I had to reject 20% of the original tasks I had received because, contrary to the instructions, some participants had just used stock photos or because the download link to the image did not work, so I reopened the HIT to get up to a hundred images.

20   This idea of ethics comes Emmanuel Levinas (1969, 1989). It offers an alternative to deontological moral theories which are based on specific content (i.e., good that transcends Being in Plato, the almighty and all-loving God in Christianity). What Levinas proposes instead is a non-systemic ethics of relations which dispenses with a need for a content-based obligation, while at the same time retaining the sense of duty. This sense

of duty is premised on the concept of the obligation to the other, which precedes any of my wishes, desires and concepts – for the simple ontological reason that the other's existence in the world precedes mine. See also my *Bioethics in the Age of New Media* (Zylinska 2009) for an attempt to extend Levinas' ethical theory to the posthumanist context.

21 It is worth citing at length from Bishop here:

> The perverse pleasures underlying these artistic gestures offer an alternative form of knowledge about capitalism's commodification of the individual, especially when both participants and viewers appear to enjoy the transgression of subordination to a work of art. If one is not to fall into the trap of merely condemning these works as reiterations of capitalist exploitation, it becomes essential to view art not as part of a seamless continuum with contemporary labor but as offering a specific space of experience where those norms are suspended and put in service of pleasure in perverse ways.... (2012, 111).

22 As Artie Vierkant explains in his widely distributed pdf titled 'The Image Object Post-Internet',

> 'Post-Internet Art' is a term coined by artist Marisa Olson and developed further by writer Gene McHugh in the critical blog 'Post Internet' during its activity between December 2009 and September 2010. Under McHugh's definition it concerns 'art responding to [a condition] described as "Post Internet" – when the Internet is less a novelty and more a banality. Perhaps ... closer to what Guthrie Lonergan described as "Internet Aware" – or when the photo of the art object is more widely dispersed [&] viewed than the object itself'. There are also several references to the idea of 'post-net culture' in the writings of Lev Manovich as early as 2001.
>
> Specifically within the context of this PDF, Post-Internet is defined as a result of the contemporary moment: inherently informed by ubiquitous authorship, the development of attention as currency, the collapse of physical space in networked culture, and the infinite

reproducibility and mutability of digital materials. (Vierkant 2010)

23 The term 'net art' (aka net.art) is associated with art made in and for the Internet, especially in its pre-platform capitalism days. Net art was irreverent and critical in spirit – towards the medium itself but also towards the very institution of art, with its celebration of objects and markets. Artists associated with the term included Vuk Ćosić, Jodi, Alexei Shulgin, Olia Lialina, Heath Bunting, Natalie Bookchin and Cornelia Sollfrank. The rhizome and nettime listserves and ensuing communities have played a key role in net art's development and recognition.

24 Distancing or alienation effect.

25 For an exposition and critique of Manovich's project of Cultural Analytics see Gary Hall, *Pirate Philosophy* (2016, 43-55).

26 Remarks made by the artist during a public conversation with Hans Ulrich Obrist at The Serpentine Galleries, October 3, 2018.

27 All links correct at the time of writing (November 2019).

Works Cited

Akten, Memo. 2017. 'Learning to See: Hello, World!', http://www.memo.tv/portfolio/learning-to-see-hello-world/

Asimov, Isaac. 1950. 'Runaround'. *I, Robot*. New York City: Doubleday.

Barrat, James. 2013. *Our Final Invention: Artificial Intelligence and the End of the Human Era*. New York: Thomas Dunne Books/St Martin's Press.

Barthes Roland. 1973. *Mythologies*. London: Paladin Books.

Batchen, Geoffrey. 2001. *Each Wild Idea: Writing Photography History*. Cambridge, MA: MIT Press.

Bazin, André. 1960. 'The Ontology of the Photographic Image'. *Film Quarterly*, Vol. 13, No. 4 (Summer): 4-9.

Benjamin, Walter. 1969. In *Illuminations*. Ed. Hannah Arendt. Trans. from the 1935 essay. New York: Schocken Books, 256-67.

Berardi, Franco 'Bifo'. 2017. *Futurability: The Age of Impotence and the Horizon of Possibility.* London: Verso. Kindle edition.

Bishop, Clare. 2012. 'Delegated Performance: Outsourcing Authenticity'. *October,* Vol. 140 (Spring). 91-112.

Boden, Margaret A. 2004. *The Creative Mind: Myths and Mechanisms.* 2nd edition. London and New York: Routledge.

Bolter, Jay David and Richard Grusin. 2002. *Remediation: Understanding New Media.* Cambridge, MA: MIT Press.

Bostrom, Nick. 2014. *Superintelligence: Paths, Dangers, Strategies.* Oxford: Oxford University Press. Kindle edition.

Bratton, Benjamin H. 2016. *The Stack: On Software and Sovereignty.* Cambridge, MA: MIT Press.

Broussard, Meredith. 2018. *Artificial Unintelligence: How Computers Misunderstand the World.* Cambridge, MA: MIT Press.

Clark, Tim. 2019. 'Trevor Paglen: From "Apple" to "Anomaly"', *British Journal of Photography,* October 10, online.

Colebrook, Claire. 2014. *Death of the PostHuman: Essays on Extinction,* Vol. 1. Ann Arbor: Open Humanities Press.

Crawford, Kate and Trevor Paglen. 2019. 'Excavating AI: The Politics of Training Sets for Machine Learning' (September 19), https://excavating.ai

Crawford, Kate and Vladan Joler. 2018. 'Anatomy of an AI System', https://anatomyof.ai/

Derrida, Jacques. 1987. *The Truth in Painting*. Chicago: University of Chicago Press.

Difallah, Djellel, Elena Filatova and Panos Ipeirotis. 2018. 'Demographics and Dynamics of Mechanical Turk Workers'. In *Proceedings of WSDM 2018: The Eleventh ACM International Conference on Web Search and Data Mining*, Marina Del Rey, CA, USA, February 5-9 (WSDM 2018), 9 pages, https://doi.org/10.1145/3159652.3159661

Dorléac, Laurence Bertrand and Jérôme Neutres. Eds. 2018. *Artistes & Robots*. Paris: Réunion des musées nationaux – Grand Palais.

Dorléac, Laurence Bertrand. 2018. 'Porquoi avoir peur des robots?'. *Artistes & Robots*. Eds. Laurence Bertrand Dorléac and Jérôme Neutres. Paris: Réunion des musées nationaux – Grand Palais, 14-35.

Dukaj, Jacek. 2017. 'Youtuberzy, ostatni artyści' (YouTubers: The Last Artists). *Gazeta Wyborcza*, Magazyn Świąteczny, November 4, http://wyborcza.pl/magazyn/7,124059,22602608,youtuberzy-ostatni-artysci-jacek-dukaj-opowiada-o-sztuce-w.html

du Sautoy, Marcus. 2019. *The Creativity Code: How AI Is Learning to Write, Paint and Think*. London: 4th Estate. Kindle edition.

Elish, Madeleine Clare. 2010. 'Representing Labor: Ten Thousand Cents and Amazon's Mechanical Turk'. *Furtherfield*, January 29, http://archive.furtherfield.org/reviews/representing-labor-ten-thousand-cents-and-amazons-mechanical-turk

Flusser, Vilém. 2000. *Towards a Philosophy of Photography*. London: Reaktion Books.

Flusser, Vilém. 2011. *Into the Universe of Technical Images*. Minneapolis: University of Minnesota Press.

Foucault, Michel. 1992. 'What is an Author?' In *Modernity and Its Discontents*, 1st ed. Eds. J. L. Marsh and J. D. Caputo. New York: Fordham University Press., 299-314.

Frosh, Paul. 2016. 'The Gestural Image: The Selfie, Photography Theory and Kinaesthetic Sociability'. In *Photomediations: A Reader*. Eds. Kamila Kuc and Joanna Zylinska. London: Open Humanities Press. 251-67.

Gibson, William. 2003. *Pattern Recognition*. New York: G. P. Putnam's Sons.

Godfrey-Smith, Peter. 2017. *Other Minds: The Octopus and the Evolution of Intelligent Life*. London: William Collins.

Google. Non-dated. Deep Dream Generator, https://deepdreamgenerator.com/

Google Arts & Culture. 2019. 'A look at Google PAIR's project, Waterfall of Meaning'.

https://artsandculture.google.com/exhibit/SAJyw84BWGgnLg

Grover, Andrea. 2011. 'Phantom Captain: Art and Crowdsourcing'. *Apexart*, https://apexart.org/exhibitions/grover.htm

Grau, Oliver, ed. 2007. *MediaArtHistories*. Cambridge, MA: MIT Press.

Hall, Gary. 2016a. *Pirate Philosophy: For a Digital Posthumanities*. Cambridge, MA: MIT Press.

Hall, Gary. 2016b. *The Uberfication of the University*. Minneapolis: University of Minnesota Press. Kindle edition.

Haugeland, John. 1997. 'What Is Mind Design?'. In *Mind Design II: Philosophy, Psychology, Artificial Intelligence*. Ed. John Haugeland. 2nd edition. Cambridge, MA: MIT Press, 1-28.

Han, Byung-Chul. 2017. *Psychopolitics: Neoliberalism and New Technologies of Power*. London: Verso. Kindle edition.

Haraway, Donna. 1998. 'Situated Knowledges: The Science Question in Feminism and the Privilege of Partial Perspective'. *Feminist Studies*, Vol. 14, No. 3 (Autumn): 575-599.

Haraway, Donna J. 2016. *Staying with the Trouble: Making Kin in the Chthulucene*. Durham: Duke University Press.

Holmes, Kevin. 2011. 'Creativity Bytes: A Brief Guide to Crowdsourced Art'. *Vice*. March 23, https://www.vice.com/en_uk/article/xyvmwd/creativity-bytes-a-brief-guide-to-crowdsourced-art

Huawei. 2018. 'Professional Phonetography at Anytime: A Look into HUAWEI P20's Master AI', June 8, https://consumer.huawei.com/en/campaign/p20-series-how-to/master-ai/

Huyghe, Pierre. 2018. *UUmwelt*. Publication accompanying Huyghe's exhibition at The Serpentine Galleries, London, October 3, 2018 – February 10, 2019.

Kant, Immanuel. 1952. *The Critique of Judgement*. Oxford: Clarendon Press.

Kelion, Leo. 2013. 'Computational photography: the snap is only the start'. *BBC News*, Technology, July 11, https://www.bbc.co.uk/news/technology-23235771

Klingemann, Mario. Non-dated. Under Destruction website. http://underdestruction.com/about/

Kogan, Gene and lkkchung. 2017. 'Neural synthesis, feature visualization, and DeepDream notes'. *GitHub*, https://github.com/ml4a/ml4a-guides/blob/master/notebooks/neural-synth.ipynb

Kurzweil, Ray. 2005. *The Singularity is Near: When Humans Transcend Biology*. New York: Viking.

Laboral: Centro de Arte y Creación Industrial. Non-dated. 'The Sheep Market', http://www.laboralcentrodearte.org/en/recursos/obras/the-sheep-market/view

Lavrador, Judicaël. 2017a. Curatorial texts for *La Belle Vie numérique! 30 artistes de Rembrandt à Xavier Veilhan*. Paris: Fondation EDF / Éditions Beaux Arts.

Lavrador, Judicaël. 2017b. 'Entretien avec Fabrice Bousteau, commissaire de l'exposition'. *La Belle Vie numérique! 30 artistes de Rembrandt à Xavier Veilhan.* Paris: Fondation EDF / Éditions Beaux Arts, 6-9.

Levinas, Emmanuel. 1969. *Totality and Infinity: An Essay on Exteriority.* Pittsburgh: Duquesne University Press.

Levinas, Emmanuel. 1989. 'Ethics as First Philosophy'. In *The Levinas Reader.* Ed. Sean Hand. Oxford: Blackwell. 75-87.

Lykkeberg, Toke. 2017. 'Art for Another Intelligence: The Work of Katja Novitskova'. In *If Only You Could See What I've Seen with Your Eyes.* Eds. Kati Ilves and Katja Novitskova. Berlin: Sternberg Press, co-published with the Center for Contemporary Arts, Estonia, 28-40.

Manovich, Lev. 2018. *AI Aesthetics.* Moscow: Strelka Press. Kindle edition.

McCarthy, Lauren. 2017. 'LAUREN. A human smart home intelligence', September, http://lauren-mccarthy.com/LAUREN

McCarthy, Lauren. 2018. 'Feeling at Home: Between Human and AI'. *Immerse* on Medium, January 8, https://immerse.news/feeling-at-home-between-human-and-ai-6047561e7f04

Milman, Oliver. 2016. 'Facebook, Google campuses at risk of being flooded due to sea level rise'. The Guardian. April 22. https://www.theguardian.com/technology/2016/apr/22/silicon-valley-sea-level-rise-google-facebook-flood-risk

Modrak, Rebekah, with Bill Anthes. 2011. *Reframing Photography: Theory and Practice*. London and New York: Routledge.

Mordvintsev, Alexander, Christopher Olah and Mike Tyka. 2015. 'Inceptionism: Going Deeper into Neural Networks'. *Google AI Blog*. June 17, https://ai.googleblog.com/2015/06/inceptionism-going-deeper-into-neural.html

Moura, Leonel. 2018. 'Robot Art: An Interview with Leonel Moura', *Arts* 7(3), 28, doi:10.3390/arts7030028.

Neutres, Jérôme. 2018. 'De l'imagination artificielle'. *Artistes & Robots*. Eds. Laurence Bertrand Dorléac and Jérôme Neutres. Paris: Réunion des musées nationaux – Grand Palais, 10-13.

New Scientist. 2017. *Machines that Think: Everything You Need to Know about the Coming Age of Artificial Intelligence*. London: John Murray. Kindle edition.

Noble, Safiya. 2018. *Algorithms of Oppression: How Search Engines Reinforce Racism*. New York: New York University Press. Kindle edition.

Novitskova, Katja. 2010. 'Foreword', *Post Internet Survival Guide*. Ed. Katja Novitskova. Berlin: Revolver Publishing, http://katjanovi.net/postinternetsurvivalguide.html

O'Connell, Mark. 2018. 'Why Silicon Valley billionaires are prepping for the apocalypse in New Zealand'. *The Guardian*. February 15. https://www.theguardian.com/news/2018/feb/15/why-silicon-valley-billionaires-are-prepping-for-the-apocalypse-in-new-zealand

Paglen, Trevor. 2014. 'Seeing Machines': posting in the Fotomuseum Wintherthur series 'Is Photography Over?'. March 13, https://www.fotomuseum.ch/en/explore/still-searching/articles/26978_seeing_machines

Paul, Christiane. 2008. *Digital Art*. 2nd edition. London: Thames & Hudson.

Peters, John Durham. 2015. *The Marvelous Clouds: Toward a Philosophy of Elemental Media*. Chicago: University of Chicago Press.

Semuels, Alana. 2018. 'The Internet Is Enabling a New Kind of Poorly Paid Hell'. *The Atlantic*, January 23, https://www.theatlantic.com/business/archive/2018/01/amazon-mechanical-turk/551192/

Simondon, Gilbert. 2016. *On the Mode of Existence of Technical Objects*. Minneapolis: Univocal.

Steyerl, Hito. 2017. *Duty Free Art: Art in the Age of Planetary Civil War*. London: Verso. Kindle edition.

Steyerl, Hito. 2018. 'Technology Has Destroyed Reality'. *New York Times*. December 5, https://www.nytimes.com/2018/12/05/opinion/technology-has-destroyed-reality.html

Stiegler, Bernard. 1998. *Technics and Time, 1: The Fault of Epimetheus*. Stanford: Stanford University Press.

Stiegler, Bernard and Irit Rogoff. 2010. 'Transindividuation', *e-flux Journal* #14, March.

Still, Arthur and Mark d'Inverno. 2016. 'A History of Creativity for Future AI Research'. Paper presented at 7th International Conference on Computational Creativity (ICCC 2016), Université Pierre et Marie Curie, Paris, France, June 27–July 1.

Stocker, Gerfried. 2017. 'The 2017 Ars Electronica Festival Theme: AI – The Other I'. In *Artificial Intelligence / Das andere Ich*. Catalogue for Ars Electronica 2017: Festival for Art, Technology, and Society. Eds. Gerfried Stocker, Christine Schöpf and Hannes Leopoldseder. Berlin: Hatje Cantz Verlag. 16–21.

Strecker, Alexander. Non-dated. 'An Urgent Look at How Artificial Intelligence Will See the World'. *LensCulture*, https://www.lensculture.com/articles/trevor-paglen-an-urgent-look-at-how-artificial-intelligence-will-see-the-world

Szegedy, Christian *et al.* 2014. 'Going Deeper with Convolutions'. arXiv:1409.4842, submitted September 17.

Tegmark, Mark. 2017. *Life 3.0: Being Human in the Age of Artificial Intelligence.* New York: Alfred A. Knopf. Kindle edition.

Temperton, James. 2015. 'Create your own DeepDream nightmares in seconds'. *Wired.* July 22, https://www.wired.co.uk/article/google-deepdream-dreamscope

Thurston, Nick. 2013. *Of the Subcontract, Or Principles of Poetic Right.* York: information as material.

Turing, A.M. 1950. 'Computing Machinery and Intelligence'. *Mind.* Vol. LIX, issue 236, 1 October: 433–460.

Vierkant, Artie. 2010. 'The Image Object Post-Internet', http://jstchillin.org/artie/pdf/The_Image_Object_Post-Internet_us.pdf

Voyce, Stephen. 2014. 'Of the Subcontract: An Interview with Nick Thurston'. *The Iowa Review.* Vol. 43:3, 94-108.

Wallace, David Foster. 2009. *This Is Water: Some Thoughts, Delivered on a Significant Occasion, about Living a Compassionate Life.* New York: Little, Brown and Company, 2009. Earlier version available online as 'Plain old untrendy troubles and emotions'. *The Guardian*, September 20, 2008, https://www.theguardian.com/books/2008/sep/20/fiction

Wershler, Darren. 2013. 'Afterword'. In *Of the Subcontract, Or Principles of Poetic Right,* Nick Thurston, York: information as material.

Zuboff, Shoshana. 2019. *The Age of Surveillance Capitalism: The Fight for a Human Future at the New Frontier of Power*. New York: Public Affairs.

Zylinska, Joanna. 2009. *Bioethics in the Age of New Media*. Cambridge, MA: MIT Press.

Zylinska, Joanna. 2014. *Minimal Ethics for the Anthropocene*. Ann Arbor: Open Humanities Press.

Zylinska Joanna. 2017. *Nonhuman Photography*. Cambridge, MA: MIT Press.

Zylinska, Joanna. 2018. *The End of Man: A Feminist Counterapocalypse*. Minneapolis: University of Minnesota Press.